Punishment of Apostasy in Islam

PUNISHMENT OF APOSTASY IN ISLAM

S.A. Rahman
Former Chief Justice of Pakistan

The Other Press
Kuala Lumpur

© 2006 The Other Press Sdn Bhd

ISBN 983-9541-49-8

First published 1972 by
Institute of Islamic Culture,
Lahore, Pakistan.

This revised edition 2006 by
The Other Press Sdn Bhd
607 Mutiara Majestic
Jalan Othman
46000 Petaling Jaya
Malaysia.
ibtkl@streamyx.com
www.ibtbooks.com

Cover design
Habibur Rahman Jalaluddin
bouncegraphics@gmail.com

Printed in Malaysia by
Academe Art & Printing Services
Kuala Lumpur

Contents

Foreword

The punishment for apostasy remains one of the most contentious issues in Islam. It has been discussed and debated for centuries by both Muslim and non-Muslim scholars. In recent decades the issue has assumed even greater significance than before largely because of the impact of human rights ideals and ideas such as freedom of religion. At the same time, the overwhelming majority of Muslims today live in societies which are heterogeneous and it is not uncommon for individuals to cross religious boundaries. Islamic resurgence which is a global phenomenon has also brought to the fore various aspects of Islamic law and its notion of crime and punishment. This has contributed to some extent to a greater scrutiny of Islam and Muslims by all and sundry—a trend that has been exacerbated no doubt by the 11 September (9/11) episode and the subsequent 'war on terror'.

All the four factors noted here—the impact of human rights and freedom of religion; religious heterogeneity *vis-à-vis* Muslims; Islamic resurgence with its emphasis upon Islamic law; and post 9/11 scrutiny of Islam and Muslims—have been responsible to a greater or lesser degree for the current attention accorded to the question of apostasy in Malaysia. Besides, as a multi-religious society par excellence, it is inevitable that Malaysia will have to grapple with controversies pertaining to religious status and identity. And some of these recent controversies have further underscored the crucial importance of understanding the issue of apostasy in the Malaysian context.

Viewed against this backdrop, it is highly commendable that The Other Press—one of the very few Malaysian publishers with a genuine commitment to the intellectual emancipation of the Muslim mind—has decided to re-publish the late S.A. Rahman's seminal work *Punishment of Apostasy in Islam*. A former Chief Justice of the Islamic Republic of Pakistan, Rahman's book first appeared in 1972. Apart from the basic thrust of his thesis which I endorse wholeheartedly, his scholarship itself is impressive. Rahman's research is thorough and comprehensive. He has examined each and every aspect of Islamic jurisprudence connected with the question of apostasy in a detailed manner. In refuting the conventional position on apostasy, his approach is analytical and scientific which is why it is so intellectually persuasive. He has succeeded in minimising the subjective element in his study. Rahman's study is also well organised and its presentation systematic. He begins by probing the Noble Qur'an's position on apostasy which is then followed by the Sunnah's (the way of the Prophet) approach to the same issue. From the Sunnah he moves to the *Khilāfah al-Rāshidah* (the Righteous Caliphate) and then to the *Fuqahā'* (the jurists) before offering some reflections on *ijtihād* (independent jurisdictional interpretation guided by the Qur'an and Sunnah) and *ijmā'* (consensus) on the question of apostasy and drawing his conclusions.

However, what is of primary importance in Rahman's work is his argument that there is no capital punishment for a Muslim who leaves his religion. He highlights various verses in the Qur'an to support his view, among them Sūrah 4:137 which says: *Those who believe, and then disbelieve, and then (again) disbelieve, and then increase in disbelief, Allah will never pardon them, nor will He guide them to the (right) way.* In explaining these lines, Rahman observes that "This is a striking pronouncement and almost conclusive against the thesis that an apostate must lose his head immediately after his defection from the faith. The verse visualises repeated apostasies and reversions to the faith, without mention of any punishment for any of these defections on this earth. The act of apostasy must, therefore, be a sin and not a crime. If he had to be killed for his very first defection, he could not possibly have a history of conversions" (p. 39). After an elaborate discussion on the writings of different Qur'anic scholars, Rahman concludes that "the Word of God clearly envisages the natural death of the apostate without any indication that he can be killed for apostasy. He will be punished only in the Hereafter ... The Qur'an includes a unique charter of liberty of conscience for mankind" (pp. 57–58).

Even the Sunnah which conservative scholars often use to justify capital punishment for apostasy does not condemn a person to death simply because of a "change of belief alone" (p. 95). Rahman points out that in cases "in which apparently such a punishment was inflicted, other factors have been found to co-exist, which would have justified action in the interest of collective security" (95). In fact, the Prophet, he stresses, "acted strictly in conformity with the letter and spirit of the Qur'an, and mere change of faith, if peaceful, cannot be visited with any punishment" (p. 95). The Righteous Caliphs followed the example of the Prophet. It was only when apostasy was combined with rebellion against the State that the death penalty was imposed.

The jurists however adopted a different approach. According to Rahman "they felt no necessity to differentiate between peaceful conversions and violent defections" (p. 145). He also shows that there was a degree of confusion in the justifications that many of the jurists provided for the death penalty.

This doctrinal perspective on apostasy which makes no distinction between 'peaceful conversions' and 'violent defections' has shaped the thinking of a significant segment of the Muslim populace. Some governments have in fact incorporated this concept of punishment for apostasy into legislation. Afghanistan, Iran and Saudi Arabia would be some examples. However, the majority of Muslim governments—perhaps influenced by the principle of freedom of religion—do not prescribe the death penalty for apostasy.

The Malaysian government would fall within this category. In any case there are very few individuals in the country who have renounced Islam. Even at the height of British colonial rule from the late nineteenth century to the middle of the twentieth century, apostasy was a rare occurrence. Nonetheless, one suspects that a huge section of the local Muslim community would acquiesce with the conventional view that apostasy should be punished with death. This would include a lot of Muslims who have had the benefit of tertiary education.

Why is there such an attitude among Malaysian Muslims? Uncritical acceptance of what the jurists regard as the religiously correct position is part of the reason. But there are also other reasons which are specific to Malaysia. The delicate demographic balance between Malays who are almost all Muslims, and the non-Malays, who are largely non-Muslim, for the most part of the last 100 years or so, coupled with the weaker economic position of the indigenous Malay community in relation to the non-indigenous, non-Malay community, especially the Chinese, have given rise to a psychology within the Malay populace as a whole which views the protection of community identity through its defining symbols as vital to its survival in its own land. And no symbol is more precious to the Malay community than its religion. This is why in the popular mind Malay often equals Islam and vice versa. The Malaysian Constitution itself defines a Malay as someone professing the Islamic faith. This intimate bond between religion and ethnic identity is perhaps unique in the Muslim world.

It explains why the very notion of leaving the religion generates extraordinary emotions within the community. To put it in stark terms, it is not just a question of forsaking one's religion; it also means abandoning one's ethnic and cultural community. In a situation where that community is deeply conscious of the challenges it faces in a multi-ethnic environment, renouncing Islam—or the act of apostasy—could even be interpreted as undermining Malay identity and integrity.

It is because of the sensitivities involved that the issue of apostasy has to be approached with wisdom and understanding by all sides. It is important that Malays and Muslims learn to appreciate—and embrace—the Qur'anic position on apostasy. As the Muslims' supreme Book of Guidance, it is the Qur'an's humane and compassionate perspective on the issue that should determine the community's stand. This has become all the more imperative in view of two seemingly paradoxical trends that we referred to at the outset: Muslims living cheek by jowl with non-Muslims in heterogeneous societies and increasing Islamic consciousness in many parts of the Muslim world.

But making allowance for apostasy does not mean encouraging it. Since it is wrong in the eyes of God, since it is, as Rahman put it, 'a sin', Muslims will try to ensure that it does not occur. By deepening and broadening the Muslims' understanding of Islam, one hopes that those who are born into Muslim families and those who convert to Islam alike will develop a profound relationship with the religion. When one really comprehends the faith and its practice, it is unlikely that one would want to abandon it, whatever the situation. This is the reason why in many Muslim countries those who seek to leave the religion, are given guidance and advice over a period of time. If, in spite of all one's endeavours, a Muslim is still adamant about renouncing the faith, the community would accept it with much regret and remorse.

By taking this approach, it is quite conceivable that Malays and other Muslims in Malaysia will be more willing to adhere to the Qur'anic perspective on apostasy. Besides, since the present demographic trend in the country favours the Malays and the economic position of the community is much stronger than it was two decades ago, it is quite possible that the community will become more sure and secure about its identity in the future. It may be in a position at that point to make a clearer distinction between ethnic identity and religious affiliation.

Malaysia's large non-Malay, non-Muslim population—about 40 percent of the total—should also make an attempt to understand the complexities of the apostasy issue from both the standpoints of Islam, on the one hand, and the Malays, on the other. They should realise for instance that though apostasy is not prohibited it is still wrong, and for that reason, Muslims are averse to classifying the renunciation of Islam as a 'right' or as a 'freedom'. This explains to some extent why almost all Muslim states in the United Nations in 1948 were reluctant to endorse the 'freedom of religion' clause in the Universal Declaration of Human Rights. This does not mean however that they did not recognise the freedom of an individual to choose her religion or even her freedom to leave the religion. It is, to reiterate, the elevation of apostasy to a right or freedom with all the positive connotation it carries which is the real problem. In Islam, a right or freedom has to be inherently good. Similarly, non-Malays should appreciate the symbiotic link between Malay identity and Islam and why apostasy in Malaysia stirs deeper emotions than in most other countries.

However, before one can understand the Malaysian situation it is important to acquire a sound grasp of the issue of apostasy itself which is why S. A. Rahman's outstanding work deserves to be read by all of us.

Dr Chandra Muzaffar

Petaling Jaya
8 August 2006

Preface to the Second Edition

The book, when first published in 1972, had a mixed response. This was perhaps to be expected considering that the author had ventured to depart, to a certain extent, from the orthodox line and to resort to a fresh orientation of the Ḥadīth literature on the subject. Some of the adverse opinions have been commented upon in the revised edition, at appropriate places. I have, however, ignored criticism based more on sentimentality and an otherwise wholly laudable enthusiasm for the Faith rather than on a fair appraisement of the thesis presented in the book, on the intellectual plane.

To both types of reviewers I am grateful, for their comments have enabled me to bring out this revised and enlarged edition. Opportunity has been taken to correct a few errors that had crept into the text and also to clarify certain points which appear to have caused some misunderstanding in the mind of one hostile critic who brought out a booklet to counter the author's views.[1] If any error still remains undetected, its responsibility is entirely mine and it would be uncharitable to ascribe it to misleading information supplied to me by those who were kind enough to discuss the subject with me or who hunted out certain references at my request. I made it a point to verify personally all such information from the sources cited as far as it was humanly possible. No opinion has been attributed to any authority, old or

---

1. Manzur Ahsan ‘Abbasi, *Jurm-i Irtidād aur us kī Islāmī Sazā*, Lahore 1974.

new, without taking care that it should be supported by chapter and verse. If some of these opinions run contrary to the general trend of the quoted author's own stand, expressed elsewhere, it may point to a logical anomaly in his thought system, but it does not mean that the opinion in question is apocryphal.

Lahore   S.A. Rahman
12 September 1977

Acknowledgements

The writer has benefited considerably from consultation and discussion with several scholars who were kind enough to hunt out references and to supply him with extremely useful information. The assistance thus received from 'Allāmah Alauddin Siddique, Vice-Chancellor, University of the Punjab, Mawlana Amin Ahsan Islahi, Mawlana M. Hanif Nadvi, Mawlana Mufti Abdul Qayyum, Advocate, M. Muhammad Ishaq Bhatti, Researcher at Institute Islamic Culture, M. Muhammad Mian Siddiqi, Research Officer, Auqaf Department, Mawlana Ihsan Ilahi Zahir, Mr Zulfiqar A Malik, Reader in Arabic University of the Punjab, Sh. Bashir Ahmad, Retired Judge, High Court, Dr S.M. Ikram and Dr Muhammad Jahangir Khan of the Research Society of Pakistan and M. Muhammad Ismail Panipati, of Lahore, and Mr Khalid Ishaq, Advocate of Karachi, and his Research Assistants, M. Siddiq Arshad and M. Abul-Hasan Muhammad Tahir, is gratefully acknowledged. The writer's thanks are also due to Mr Abdul Majid Khan for typing out the manuscript for him and to the officials of the Punjab University Library and the Punjab Public Library (Oriental Section) for the unfailing courtesy and promptitude with which they attended to his requests for books of reference. For the English rendering of the Qur'anic verses, the writer has relied in the main on the translation of the Qur'an by the late Muhammad Marmaduke Pickthall, changing only a word here or there.

Mr Ashraf Darr of the Institute of Islamic Culture, Lahore, got the typescript prepared for publication and saw the book through the press in all its stages with his usual thoroughness and took great pains over the proofs. I gratefully acknowledge his valuable assistance in this regard.

7 May 1972
S.A. Rahman

Introduction

The State of Pakistan is the end-result of a historical process which started with the first Muslim invasion of this subcontinent. Various factors, political, economic, social, cultural and religious, operated on and entered into the structure of the Muslim nation which emerged, in 1947, as a unique ideological State, comprising two units separated by a thousand miles of hostile Indian territory. Its dominating inspiration, however, came from the religious consciousness of the Muslims of the subcontinent, which crystallised into an ardent longing for a terrestrial base for the working out of what was regarded as a Divine Plan of action in the sociopolitical sphere. Implementation of the Islamic values of life was declared to be the objective before the Founding Fathers of Pakistan by a formal Constitutional Instrument drawn up finally in 1956. The Constitution of 1956 was, however, superseded by the Martial Law regime in 1958 and, four years later, the Constitution of 1962 was promulgated by a Presidential Decree, under the protective umbrella of Martial Law. The latest constitutional instrument in the field is the Constitution of the Islamic Republic of Pakistan, 1973. This Constitution expressly declares in its Article 2 that Islam shall be the State religion of Pakistan. Article 227 thereof provides that all existing laws shall be brought into conformity with the injunctions of Islam as laid down in the Holy Qur'an and the Sunnah and that no law shall be enacted which is repugnant to such injunctions. Whatever may have been the political overtones or undertones of these constitutional dispensations, they respected the ambition of the majority Muslim community to order their lives in accordance with the dictates of the Qur'an and the Sunnah, while ensuring cultural and religious autonomy and fundamental political equality to the non-Muslim minorities.

Though some political parties have sponsored schemes of a more equitable distribution of the means of production and wealth under the undefined terminology of "Islamic Socialism", none has denied the efficacy of the religious motivation in the life of the Muslim community and, except for a small group of extremists, even the leftist parties have professed anxiety for pressing into service the principles of Islamic social justice. The question therefore, as to what sort of polity the fundamentals of Islam envisage is very much a live issue in the context of our present-day politics.

The non-Muslim resident in Pakistan, since its inception, were assured time and again by the Qā'id-i A'ẓam Muhammad Ali Jinnah, that they would have all the fundamental rights guaranteed to them, on a basis of equality with the members of the majority community and that they may even expect to receive generous rather than merely egalitarian treatment. These non-Muslims are neither *dhimmīs* nor *mustā'mins* in the technical sense of Muslim jurisprudence. Their position is assimilable to that of *mu'āhids*—the beneficiaries of a binding pact. There is august precedent available in Muslim history for this kind of grating equation for certain State purposes, subject to the different communities enjoying full liberty of conscience and autonomy of action in the religious field, with the overriding reservation that the Head of the State must belong to the numerically predominant community. The Prophet (on him be peace) had entered into such a pact with the Jewish and Christian tribes of Madīnah, after his migration from Makkah (the *Hijrah*).[1] The Qā'id-i A'ẓam was, therefore, essentially right in holding out an assurance of this character to those non-Muslim who owed unquestioning allegiance to the State of Pakistan.

With a mixed population such as we have in Pakistan, the problem of inter-communal harmony assumes importance. Freedom of conscience, the right to profess as well as propagate one's own faith and to safeguard one's religious institutions, consistently with law and morality, would be regarded as the inviolable right of every community in the modern world. The position of the proselyte, if he happens to belong to the majority community, would present a testing ground of good faith and fair play in inter-communal relations. Unfortunately our *fiqh* compendiums do not enter on an analytical study of this problem, in the light of the Qur'anic injunctions and authentic Sunnah, and no distinction apparently exists in the minds of the old jurists between apostasy simpliciter and apostasy combined with treason or severance of allegiance to the State. It is tacitly assumed that every apostate from Islam deserves the death penalty, not merely as a renegade from the true faith, but also as a *muḥārib*—an active rebel. Such a doctrine could have far-reaching repercussions in the socio-political sphere and might invite retaliatory legislation from countries where the Muslims happen to be in a minority. Eventually such a legislative war might put an end to all missionary activity in support of Islam.

The image of Islam presented by some of the non-Muslim Western scholars strikes a humble student of the Qur'an, like the

---

1. Dr Muhammad Hamidullah, *Siyāsī Wathīqah Jāt* (Urdu translation, pp. 19–24).

present writer, to be a crude caricature of its liberal humanitarian teachings. Majid Khadduri's appraisal of the Islamic Law on the subject of apostasy leads him to conclude that "both jurists and theologians agree that apostasy constitutes a violation of law, punishable both in this world and the next. Not only is the person denied salvation in the next world but he is liable to capital punishment by the State."[2] Samuel M. Zwemer, Christian missionary in Egypt, claims that there are so few converts from amongst Muslims to Christianity, in spite of prodigious missionary efforts, because the sword of Damocles is always hanging over their heads in the shape of the death sentence, if they commit apostasy. He quotes from Dr Andrew Watson's *History of the American Mission in Egypt (1854–1894)* an assertion that all seventy-five converts to Christianity, from among Muslims, were subject to persecution "because the idea of personal liberty—freedom of conscience—has no place in Muslim Law, whether religious or civil."[3] Such distortions of the clear Qur'anic injunction of there being no compulsion in religion (*Lā ikrāha fī al-Dīn*) are, however, made possible (speaking with all respect) by uncritical generalisations of concrete decisions in our history, by our own scholars and jurisconsults. By and large, our orthodox *fuqahā'* (jurists) have taken the inelastic line that the punishment for apostasy in Islam is death. Echoes of this view are to be heard in the writings of some of our modern savants as well. Only two such instances may suffice to illustrate my point.

In the estimation of a reputed Muslim scholar, apostasy "constitutes a politico-religious rebellion". He sums up his views in these terms:

---

2. Majid Khadduri, *War and Peace in the Law of Islam*, pp. 149–151.
3. Samuel M. Zwemer, *The Law of Apostasy in Islam*, Chapter I, pp. 19–20.

The sayings and doings of the Prophet, the decisions and practice of the Caliph Abū Bakr, the consensus of the opinion of the Companions of the Prophet and all the later Muslim jurisconsults, and even certain indirect verses of the Qur'an, all prescribe capital punishments for an apostate.[4]

Working out the logical consequences of a similar stand, another modern scholar, who also heads a religio-political party in Pakistan, expresses himself on the incidents of an Islamic State, with this pronouncement:

To my mind the solution lies in this (*wa Allāhu al-muwaffiqu li al-ṣawāb* = God alone leads us into conformity with what is right)— whenever the Islamic revolution is successful, the Muslim population will be notified that those who renounce Islam by declaration of a different faith or by their actions, but desire to remain subjects of the State, shall, within a year of the notification, proclaim themselves publicly to be non-Muslims and to be outside the pale of the Muslim community. After the expiry of this period, those born in Muslim households would be deemed to be Muslims bound by all the Islamic Laws. They will be compelled to carry out all obligations and observe all injunctions of the Faith. Thereafter if one of them leaves the fold of Islam, he shall be put to death. After the issue of such a notification, all efforts shall be made to save as many of the Muslim-born children as possible from falling into lap of disbelief, and those not amenable to the process of conservation shall have to be cut off from the social organism with a determined hand though a heavy heart. After this purge, the Islamic polity shall be inaugurated with the support of such Muslims as are devoted to Islam.[5]

This solemn pronouncement conjures up a vision of the shape of things to come which the present writer ventures to

---

4. Dr M. Hamidullah, *Muslim Conduct of State* (1973 ed.), Part III, Chapter VI, pp. 180–181.
5. S. Abul A'la Mawdudi, *Murtadd kī Sazā Islāmī Qānūn min.* pp. 75–76.

think, will not commend itself to those thinking individuals who believe in Islam as a living force for all times and climes. Such writings would of course be avidly seized upon by censorious Western scholars as grist for their polemical mill.

In 1924–1925, the question of punishment for apostasy was the subject of controversy between the Daily *Hamdard* of the late Mawlana Muhammad Ali Jauhar and the Daily *Zamīndār* of Lahore, edited by the late Mawlana Zafar Ali Khan. This was occasioned by the stoning to death at Kabul, for alleged apostasy, of one Nimatullah, a member of the Qadiyani section of the Ahmadi sect. M. Muhammad 'Ali Jawhar had sponsored the thesis that Islam did not sanction any punishment for apostasy as such and from the side of the *Zamīndār*, this proposition was vehemently contested. The writer had access to the articles published on the subject in the *Zamīndār* through the courtesy of Dr S.M. Ikram and Dr M. Jahangir Khan of the Research Society of Pakistan, Lahore. The three articles written by M. Muhammad Ali Jauhar have been reproduced in the Daily *Payghām-i Ṣulḥ* of Lahore out of which two, *viz.*, those published in the issue of the paper dated 4 March and 11 March 1925 are relevant to our theme. The file of this paper was placed at the writer's disposal very kindly by the present Editor of that paper. This file also contained some other relevant material which has been commented upon in the sequel.

From the point of view of the solidarity and integrity of the Islamic community, the question assumes vital importance when we recall to mind the historic fact that the so-called sects of Muslims have been too prone to condemn one another as disbelievers, on the basis of slight deviations from the orthodox position, in respect of doctrine or practice. The grounds on which a person could be declared to be a *kāfir* (disbeliever) appear to be vast and varied and some idea of the wide field they cover may be obtained from a study of *faṣl al-thālith* of *bāb al-awwal* of al-Sāmarā'ī's *Aḥkām al-Murtadd*.[6]

With this background of facts in mind, I have ventured to examine *de novo*, in the light of the fundamental sources of Islamic Law, the question whether apostasy simpliciter, without any political strings attached, is at all punishable in Islam and, if so, whether it is possible to spell out of the historical precedents, cited in support of the death penalty for change of faith, any general rule laying down the measure of such punishment. I was encouraged to embark on this venture by the stimulating sixth lecture of the late 'Allāmah Dr Sir Muhammad Iqbal, headed as "The Principle of Movement in the Structure of Islam". Among other profound observations the following inspiring comment occurs therein:

> The claim of the present generation of Muslim liberals to reinterpret the foundational legal principles, in the light of their own experience and the altered conditions of modern life is, in my opinion, perfectly justified. The teaching of the Qur'an that life is a process of progressive creation necessitates that each generation, guided but unhampered by the work of its predecessors, should be permitted to solve its own problems.[7]

What follows is a humble attempt in the direction indicated by 'Allāmah Iqbal, but neither finality nor infallibility is claimed for the opinions expressed herein: *Wa Allāh a'lam bi al-ṣawāb* (And God is the best knower of the truth).

---

6. Al-Sāmarā'ī, *Aḥkām al-Murtadd*, pp. 77–137.
7. Dr Sir Muhammad Iqbal, *Six Lectures on the Reconstruction of Religious Thought in Islam*, p. 168.

CHAPTER I

Apostasy and the Qur'an

Section I—The Spirit of the Qur'an

The Arabic equivalent for apostasy is *riddah* or *irtidād* from the root *radd* which, among other connotations, has the meaning "to retreat, to retire, to withdraw from or fall back from". In the context of Muslim *fiqh* (jurisprudence) it is equated with renunciation or abandonment of Islam by one who professes the Islamic faith. The apostate is called *murtadd*. According to Muslim jurists, apostasy may be committed with reference to belief, word or deed, or even by failure to observe certain obligatory practices. The person concerned must have attained majority, should be in full possession of his senses and should have acted voluntarily, if he is to be condemned as an apostate. An elaborate discussion of the antecedents of apostasy would be beyond the scope of our subject. An adequate summary of the jurists' views on this subject found in the second and third *fuṣūl* (sections) of the first chapter (*bāb al-awwal*) of al-Sāmarā'ī's *Aḥkām al-Murtadd*.[1]

In the Introduction to his book, al-Sāmarā'ī observes as follows:

In the Book [the Qur'an] I found sometimes "*al-riddah*" mentioned expressly and sometimes by import. I followed up the verses in the

---

1. Al-Sāmarā'ī, *Aḥkām al-Murtadd*, pp. 77–137.

various commentaries and I arrived at the conclusion that the punishment of the apostate (and that is death) is not to be bond in the Book but finds mention in the Sunnah only.[2]

This view is fairly representative of the opinions of scholars who have written on the subject. There is absolutely no mention in the Qur'an of any punishment for apostasy to be inflicted in this world. In the article headed "*Murtadd*" in the *Encyclopaedia of Islam* (Leyden, 1932),[3] Professor Heffening has acknowledged this fact expressly.

Dr Muhammad Hamidullah, in his *Muslim Conduct of State*, has referred to some "indirect verses of the Qur'an" as bearing on the point of punishment for apostasy, *viz.,* al-Mā'idah: verse 54, and al-Aḥzāb: verse 57, but it is difficult to agree with him that these verses can be pressed into service for sustaining the capital sentence for apostasy. For his main thesis, M. Abul A'la Mawdudi has relied on the Qur'anic verses:

فَإِن تَابُواْ وَأَقَامُواْ ٱلصَّلَوٰةَ وَءَاتَوُاْ ٱلزَّكَوٰةَ فَإِخْوَٰنُكُمْ فِى ٱلدِّينِ وَنُفَصِّلُ ٱلْأَيَـٰتِ لِقَوْمٍ يَعْلَمُونَ ۞ وَإِن نَّكَثُوٓاْ أَيْمَـٰنَهُم مِّنۢ بَعْدِ عَهْدِهِمْ وَطَعَنُواْ فِى دِينِكُمْ فَقَـٰتِلُوٓاْ أَئِمَّةَ ٱلْكُفْرِ إِنَّهُمْ لَآ أَيْمَـٰنَ لَهُمْ لَعَلَّهُمْ يَنتَهُونَ ۞

(9:11–12)

He has interpreted these verses in a sense which is at variance with their generally accepted connotation. According to him, they should be rendered as: "Then if they repent (of their disbelief) and observe prayer and pay the *zakāh*, they are your brethren in faith. We explain Our injunctions for a people who have knowledge. But if they break their oaths, after their covenant (*ie.*, their covenant to accept Islam) and make your *dīn*

---

2. *Ibid.*, p. 12.
3. Vol. III, Part Z, p. 737.

the target of their taunts, then fight these leaders of disbelief, for their oaths cannot be depended upon—maybe that they shall thus desist."[4] He construes the word *'ahd* as meaning a "covenant to accept Islam". This construction, generally speaking, is not borne out by the well known commentaries, published in the Indo-Pak subcontinent or abroad. Mr Marmaduke Pickthall translates the word *'ahd* as "treaty" which obviously does not bear on change of faith. Mawlana Shah 'Abdul Qadir,[5] Mawlana Ashraf 'Ali Thanawi,[6] Mahmud al-Hasan Deobandi,[7] Mawlana Shabbir Ahmad 'Uthmani, Mawlana Shah Muhammad Ahmad Rida Khan Barelvi,[8] Sayyid Muhammad Naim-ud-Din Muradabadi, Mawlana Abul Kalam Azad,[9] M. Muhammad 'Ali,[10] Mr 'Abdullah Yūsuf 'Alī,[11] Nawab Siddiq Hasan,[12] take the term *'ahd* as equivalent to a political pact and, in their comments on these verses, give the history of the agreements between the Muslims and the disbelieving Quraysh, starting from the Peace of Ḥudaybiyah, as the background for their revelation. The standard exegetical works of al-Bayḍāwī,[13] al-Zamakhsharī,[14] al-Jaṣṣāṣ,[15] Fakhr al-

---

4. S. Abul A'la Mawdudi, *Murtadd kī Sazā Islāmī Qānūn min*, pp.
5. Shah 'Abdul Qadir, *Tafsīr Mūḍiḥ al-Qur'ān*, p. 172.
6. M. Ashraf 'Ali Thanawi, *Mu'jiz Numā' Ḥamā'il Sharīf* (with Urdu translation), pp. 299–300; also his *Bayān al-Qur'ān* (Urdu commentary), Vols. IV, V and VI, pp. 92–93, 98–99.
7. *Qur'ān Majīd Mutarjam wa Muḥashshah*, Urdu translation by M. Mahmud al-Hasan, and marginal commentary by M. Shabbir Ahmad Uthman, pp. 242–243.
8. *Al-Qu'ān al-Ḥakīm*, with Urdu translation by Muftī Shah Muhammad Ahmad Rida Khan—marginal commentary by Sayyid M. Na'ium-ud-Din, pp. 271–272.
9. Abul Kalam Azad, *Tarjumān al-Qur'ān*, II, 77.
10. M. Muhammad 'Ali, *English translation and commentary of the Holy Qur'ān, with Arabic Text*, Sixth Edition, 1973, pp. 383–389.
11. 'Abdullah Yūsuf 'Alī, *English translation with commentary of the Holy Qur'ān*, I, 436–437, 441.
12. Nawab Siddiq Hasan Khan, *Fatḥ al-Bayān*, IV, 86.
13. *Tafsīr Bayḍāwī* with *Tafsīr Jalālayn* of al-Suyūṭī, and *al-Muḥallā* on margin, I, 340.

Dīn al-Rāzī,[16] and al-Ālūsī,[17] too, take an identical view so far as the word *'ahd* is concerned. But while interpreting these verses and the next, all except al-Jaṣṣāṣ refer to the lesser known alternative reading of *aymānahum* (their oaths) as *īmānahum* (their faiths) and indicate that the suggested alternative would require the rendering to be: "And if they break what they have said in the oath of allegiance as part of their faith or as part of their promise to fulfil covenants." Al-Rāzī and Alūsī, however, give distinct preference to the construction based on political covenants, for, as al-Rāzī observes, "the verse was revealed in respect of those who broke their covenants," and he rejects the alternative reading of *īmānahum* as not in conformity with the context. Al-Zamakhsharī, it may be noted, also translates the identical words "*nakathū aymānahum*" occurring in the following verse as referring to their political agreement. Al-Bayḍāwī adopts the reading "*īmān*" for "*aymān*", only in the expression "*innahum lā aymāna lahum*" and he too equates the words "*nakathū aymānahum*" in the next verse with the breach of faith in respect of covenants with the Prophet and the Muslims. The *Tafsīr al-Manār*[18] in its exposition of these verses records that they clearly relate to the *mushrikīn* (polytheists) of Arabia who had entered into covenants with the faithful but had deliberately broken them and adds that the generality of the injunction embodied in them would comprehend all those whose relations with the Muslims can be assimilated to those with the *mushrikīn*. Mawlana Mawdudi, therefore, does not have the sanction of any clear-cut authority behind his interpretation which is also inconsistent with the theme of Sūrah al-Tawbah.

14. Al-Zamakhsharī, *Al-Kashshāf*, II, 251 *et seq.*
15. Al-Jaṣṣāṣ, *Aḥkām al-Qur'ān*, III, 105.
16. Al-Rāzī, *Al-Tafsīr al-Kabīr*, IV, 416.
17. Al-Ālūsī, *Rūḥ al-Ma'ānī*, X, 42, 57, 58.
18. Rashīd Riḍā, *Tafsīr al-Manār*, X, 187–191.

The object of the fighting against infidels specified at the end of the verse is to make them "desist" (from their actions). This object accords with the preferred construction. If the persons concerned were to be killed for apostasy, there should have been no question of an attempt to making them "desist" from their course. The subsequent verses establish that the disbelievers had repeatedly broken their covenants and had taken the initiative in the fighting. The directive given is to fight them to ensure peace and order and not to slay them, par excellence, as al-Bayḍāwī explicitly clarifies.

The position that emerges, then, is that it is not possible to spell out the death penalty for apostasy from a study of the Qur'an alone. Indeed, if dispassionate consideration is given to the Qur'anic text, without preconceived notions, it will be found that the punishment of the apostate is postponed to the Hereafter. In matters concerning the individual conscience, the Qur'an places no fetters on free choice. The appeal of the Qur'an is to history, observation and reason, in support of its invitation to the path of faith and rectitude. Even to contestants of the truth, it issues a challenge to adduce evidence to sustain their assertions.

قُلْ هَاتُواْ بُرْهَـٰنَكُمْ إِن كُنتُمْ صَـٰدِقِينَ

Say: Bring forth your proof, if you are truthful. (2:111)

This rational approach runs like a golden thread throughout the fabric of the Qur'anic teachings. To emphasise the importance of the deliberative function, the Qur'an declares in ringing terms of admonition:

> And be not like those who say 'We hear,' but they hear not. Surely the worst of beasts in the sight of Allah are the deaf and the dumb, who have no sense. (8:21–22)

To attribute an intention to the Divine Scheme of compelling renegades from the true faith to resume their allegiance to God and the Prophet on pain of being killed, would apparently run counter to the letter and spirit of the various directives and admonitions included in the Qur'an, pertinent to this question. The call to the Way of the Lord is to be made with wisdom and fair exhortation and people are to be reasoned with "in the better way" (16:125). Even the false gods of the opponents of the faith are to be immune from abusive references. Says the Qur'an:

> Revile not those unto whom they pray besides Allah, lest they, out of spite, revile Allah through ignorance. Thus unto every people have We made their doings seem fair. Then unto their Lord is their return; and He will inform them of what they used to do." (6:109)

If war (only defensive wars are permitted) is to be resorted to, its objective must be the establishment of the fundamental human right of liberty of conscience. In Sūrah al-Baqarah, it is solemnly declared:

> Fight in the way of Allah against those who fight against you, but do not transgress. Surly Allah loves not the transgressors. And slay them wherever you find them and drive them out of the places whence they drove you out, for persecution is worse than slaughter. And fight not with them near the Sacred Mosque until they first attach you there, but if they fight you, then slay them. Such is the requital for disbelievers. But if they desist, then lo! Allah is Forgiving, Merciful. And fight them until persecution is no more and religion is only for Allah. But it they desist, then let there be no hostility except against wrongdoers. (2:190–193)

Condign punishment in this world is reserved only for those who are out to fight the faithful and disrupt the social order. Their case is dealt with in Sūrah al-Mā'idah in the following words:

> The only reward of those who make war upon Allah and His Messenger and strive to create disorder in the land, will be that they will be slain or crucified or have their hands and feet on

alternate sides cut off, or will be expelled from the land. Such will be their degradation in the world, and in the Hereafter theirs will be an awful doom, save those who repent before you overpower them. For know that Allah is Forgiving, Merciful (5:33–34).

Duress or coercion in matters of belief does not enter into the composition of the social system envisaged by the Qur'an. Clear guidance in a truly humanitarian spirit of tolerance is given to the Muslims in this field in several verses which recognise the existence of a pluralistic milieu, though of course a categorical distinction is drawn between those who follow the Straight Path and those who are misguided and have become impervious to the signs of God. The latter are warped of the punishment awaiting them in the Hereafter. The realistic and humanistic stance of the Qur'an is amply illustrated by the following, among other, commandments:

1. Lo! those who believe (in that which is revealed unto thee, Muḥammad), and those who are Jews, and Christians and Sabeans believes in Allah and the Last Day and does right—surely their reward is with their Lord and no fear shall come upon them, nor shall they grieve. (2:62)
2. Lo! those who disbelieve and die while they are disbelievers, on them shall be the curse of Allah and of angels and men combined. (2:161)
3. There is no compulsion in religion. Surely the right direction is henceforth distinct from error. And he who rejects false deities and believes in Allah has grasped a firm handlehold which will never break. And Allah is Hearer, Knower. (2:256)

This (verse 256) is one of the most important verses of the Qur'an, containing a charter of freedom of conscience unparalleled in the religious annals of mankind and deserves detailed discussion. It is with regret mingled with perturbation that one notices attempts made by Muslim scholars themselves to whittle down its broad humanistic meaning by imposing limitations on its scope, dictated by exigencies of theological controversies that arose in the course of our history. By this means it was intended to correlate the word of God with what was understood to be the Prophet's Sunnah or to reconcile it with inferences drawn from historical precedents whose full background was seldom explored.

Some of the exegetists of the Qur'an[19] cite the opinion that this verse had been abrogated by other verses such as: "O Prophet, strive against the disbelievers and the hypocrites. Be harsh with them" (9:73); "O ye who believe! Fight those of the disbelievers who are near to you and let them find harshness (hardness) in you" (9: 12); and "Say unto the wandering Arabs who were left behind: 'You will be called against a folk of mighty prowess to fight them until they surrender'" (48:16). But the majority of the commentators negative the theory of abrogation and prefer the reports which suggest that the verse under examination was revealed with reference to the case of an Anṣār woman who had vowed that if her son survived, she would make him a Jew. The son had joined the Jewish tribe of Banū al-Naḍīr in Madīnah, but when this tribe was banished there from for their perfidy, the Anṣār tried to detain the boy and to convert him to Islam. This was not allowed to be done because of this revelation. An alternative version connects it with the case of an Anṣār named Ḥaṣīn whose two sons were Christian. He consulted the Prophet (peace be upon him) who forbade him from his intention to force them into the Islamic fold. Still another version links the verse with the case of a slave from the

---

19. Siddiq Hasan Khan, *op. cit.*, I, 426; Abī Bakr ibn al-'Arabī, *Aḥkām al-Qur'ān*, Part I, pp. 232; *et seq.*; Abī Ḥayyān, *Baḥr al-Muḥīṭ*, II, 281; al-Ālūsī, *op. cit.*, III, 12–13; al-Zamakhsharī, *op. cit.*, I, 303 and 387; al-Bayḍāwī, *Tafsīr* on the margin of the Qur'an (Egypt, 1344 H), first half, p. 53.

Ahl al-Kitāb (People of the Scripture) whose adherence to his own faith was respected under this injunction. Finally, it was given out as the opinion of some that it was meant to cover the case of those People of the Book who had submitted to the Muslims and had agreed to pay *jizyah* (poll-tax).[20]

The wording of the verse is perfectly general and the versions about its *Sha'n al-Nuzūl* (occasion for revelation) cannot detract from the full effect of the eternal principles of human polity, laid down therein. It would be pertinent to consider, in this connection, the acute observations of Shah Waliyullah in his *Al-Fawz al-Kabīr fī Uṣūl al-Tafsīr*.[21] In Chapter III, headed "*Asbāb-i Nuzūl*", he says:

> Knotty problems arise in connection with the question of *asbāb-i nuzūl* (grounds of revelations). This is due to differences in technical expressions used by earlier and later exponents. From the statements of the Companions and those who followed them, the conclusion can be drawn that when these venerable persons say that an *āyah* was revealed in the context of such and such incidents, then it is not intended to confine its application to that incident which might have occurred during the Prophet's time and occasioned the revelation. These venerable persons were in the habit of mentioning incidents or situations in the Prophet lifetime or thereafter which, according to their view, were linked with a verse. This did not necessarily lead to the inference that the verse in question would wholly and exclusively pertain to such incident or situation. On the contrary, the verse should be held to convey the commandment contained therein, generally.

---

20. Ibn 'Abbās, *Tafsīr*, with al-Suyūṭī's *Lubab al-Nuqūl*, p. 114; al-Suyūṭī, *Al-Durr al-Manthūr*, I, 329–30; Abī Ḥayyān, *op. cit.*, II, 281 *et seq.*; al-Ālūsī, *op. cit.*, III, 12–13; al-Zamakhsharī, *op. cit.*, I, 303 and 387 *et seq.*; Siddiq Hasan Khan, *op. cit.*, I, 426 *et seq.*
21. Urdu translation by Muhammad Salim Abdullah, pp. 96–97.

Some extraordinary observations are, however, to be met with in the interpretation of this important verse in learned commentaries of exegetists whose erudition, piety and scholarship are universally acknowledged and above question. For instance, no less a personality than Shah Waliyullah, in his Persian translation of the Qur'an, the *Fath al-Rahmān,* while giving the generally accepted rendering of the verse in the main context, adds a marginal gloss which reads: "That is to say, the reasoned guidance of Islam has become manifest. Thereafter, so to speak, there is no compulsion, although, in sum, there may be coercion."[22] In other words, coercion is justified by a good cause and, in such a case, what appears to be compulsion is no compulsion at all. With the highest reverence for the great savant it would take a lot of persuasion to accept this kind of sophistication as consistent with the clarity and forthrightness of the *Kitāb al-Mubīn* (the Explicit Book). There is no indication in the text that the words are to be understood in a restricted or qualified sense, nor would the *Sha'n al-Nuzūl* reports justify that course. Such an interpretation can perhaps be attributed to the unconscious pressure of orthodox tradition.

Kindred comments are included in the *Fath al-Bayān* of Nawab Siddiq Hasan Khan.[23] According to one view, mentioned therein, one should not say of a person converted to Islam under the shadow of the sword, that he was compelled to the Faith for "there is no compulsion in Religion"! Another construction cited therein (also noticed by al-Ālūsī in *Rūh al-Ma'ānī*[24] and by Abī Hayyān in *Bahr al-Muhīt*[25]) confines the verse to the People of the Scriptures, who submitted to the Muslims and agreed to pay

---

22. Shah Waliyullah, *Fath al-Rahmān* (1312 H), p. 57.
23. I, 426 *et seq.*, and 340.
24. III, 12–13
25. II, 281.

jizyah (poll-tax) but excludes the idolaters from its scope. In the case of the latter, only two alternatives are said to be open—Islam or the sword—on the authority of al-Sha'bī, Ḥasan, Qatādah and al-Ḍaḥḥāk. Siddiq Hasan Khan recognises the accepted principle of exegesis that regard will be had to the generality of the words and not to the particular circumstances that occasioned the revelation, but claims that the general is here particularised by other verses which sanctioned the use of force against *ahl al-ḥarb* (fighters) among disbelievers. He has not specified the verses he had in mind but, in any event, the argument is specious. For those who fight the Muslims fall in a different category from those who differ from the faithful, without being aggressive.

Ibn al-'Arabī in his *Aḥkām al-Qur'ān* [26] is much more categorical in his assertions. He declares dogmatically that to compel to the truth is part of the Faith, on the authority of a *ḥadīth*: "I have been commanded to fight people till they recite the declaration of faith (*Lā ilāha illā Allāh* = there is no god but Allah)," which he considers to have been derived from the Qur'anic verse: "And fight them until persecution is no more and religion is for Allah alone" (8:39; 2:193). Issue may be fairly joined with the learned commentator on the point of these verses supplying the authority for the reported *ḥadīth*, for the verses clearly and explicitly enjoin fighting to end religious persecution and lend no support to the theory of justification of force even in the interest of truth. Ibn al-'Arabī puts forward the specious argument that "the Prophet was charged with the mission to invite people to the Straight Path and to establish *Ḥujjat Allāh* and that, after a time, God changed his condition from one of a victim of persecution to that of security and from weakness to

---

26. Part I, pp. 232 *et seq.*

strength and provided him with strong helpers and commanded him to resort to the sword for the fulfillment of his mission." This view would imply that the injunction against use of force in the matter of religion was limited to the initial period of weakness of the Muslims and its non-observance would be permissible from a position of strength and prosperity. There is no warrant for such a conclusion to be found in any Qur'anic verse and indeed the ethical plane of such argumentation is too obvious to require comment. Clearly when the Banū al-Naḍīr were being banished from Madīnah, the Anṣār woman son, who was with them, could have been very easily detained by the Muslims, for the Banū al-Naḍīr would have been in no position to resist. But God's infinite Wisdom had prescribed otherwise and the Muslims submitted to the Divine Ordinance. The circumstances surrounding the saying ascribed to the Prophet are not brought out in the *Aḥkām al-Qur'ān* and, for all we know, it may have relevance to the case of active enemies of Islam.

There is good authority for the opposite view. While discussing the contribution of Imām Ibn Taymiyyah to *fiqh*, Professor Abū Zahrah of Egypt, in his book *Imām Ibn Taymiyyah*,[27] summarises the Imām's opinion in the following terms:

> On the first question as to whether it is permissible to fight the disbelievers on the ground of their disbelief or on that of their tyranny and transgression, the Imām refers to two schools of thought among the *'Ulamā'*. The first school holds that according to Imām Mālik, Imām Aḥmad bin Ḥanbal, Imām Abū Ḥanīfah and others, and the majority of *'Ulamā'* and *A'immah*, fighting with disbelievers is allowed only if they are bent upon oppression and tyranny. From this opinion it follows that war with infidels is not permissible in any other circumstances. Consequently fighting can

---

27. Urdu translation by Na'ib Husain Naqwi, pp. 554 *et seq.*

be resorted to as a defensive measure or in response to aggression, even if it turns out to be a case of emergency. But in such a fight only the active combatants or their inciters will be killed, and women, anchorites and disabled or old people, who neither participate in the fighting nor exhort others to do so, will not be slain. In brief, the disbeliever who does not take up arms, does not urge others to fight and is not guilty of any hostile act in connection with the war shall not be put to death.

The second school is of the opinion that war with the disbelievers is grounded on their disbelief. That means that fighting is obligatory with them simply because they are infidels and not because they are inclined to tyranny. This is the creed of Imām al-Shāfiʿī. Therefore, under this principle, every disbeliever who has attained majority and discretion would be deserving of capital punishment, irrespective of whether he is capable of fighting or not, whether he is himself on the war path or not and whether he is actively assisting his comrades (the disbelievers) to pursue the fight or not.

In this regard, Imām Ibn Taymiyyah considers the first opinion, *viz.,* the opinion of the majority, to be correct and, in support of his position cites authorities from the Qur'an and the Sunnah.

The authorities referred to by the Imām include the very verse under discussion (*Lā ikrāha fī al-dīn*), which, he says, is neither abrogated not circumscribed in scope by any incident or other consideration. He also cites the verses: "Fight in the way of Allah against those who fight against you, but begin not hostilities" (2:190) and "Fight with them until persecution is no more and religion is only for Allah" (2:193). Reliance is also placed by him on Traditions showing that the Prophet had forbidden the slaying of women because of their lack of capacity to fight and had never forced any war captives to adopt Islam. He points out that all wars of the Prophet were defensive in character—a subject he expounds in his *Risālat al-Qitāl.*

Shaykh Maḥmūd Shaltūt, in his *Tafsīr al-Qur'ān al-Ḥakīm*,[28] also clearly endorses the view of Imām Ibn Taymiyyah by saying that disbelief alone cannot make it lawful to kill a disbeliever, but there must be an element of aggression and hostile transgression with it to justify action.

In the *Baḥr al-Muḥīṭ*[29] the view of Imām Mālik and Kalbī that this *āyah* is not confined to the *ahl al-qitāl* but embraces within its pale all disbelievers, who may have elected to pay *jizyah*, also finds a place. What is highly significant and important is that Abī Ḥayyān, *inter alia*, reproduces the more logically consistent interpretation (which is in conformity with the letter and spirit of the Qur'an) that even a person who renounces Islam for another religion cannot be compelled to revert to his former faith. Then follows the opinion attributed to Abū Muslim and Qifāl that the meaning of the verse is that God has not based matters of *īmān* (faith) on compulsion and force but on voluntary and free choice, for the arguments in favour of *Tawḥīd* (Divine Unity) have become manifest by full exposition. After that, there is no excuse left for disbelief so that one may say that the disbeliever should be obliged to adopt the faith and be bound to it. But that is not permissible in this world trial and tribulation, for coercion and constraint for the faith negative the reality of trial and testing. This reasoning is also adverted to by al-Zamakhsharī in *Al-Kashshāf*[30] and by al-Ālūsī in his *Rūḥ al-Ma'ānī*.[31] The former cites the Qur'anic verse:

> If thy Lord had willed (enforced His Will), all who are in the earth would have believed together; would thou compel men until they are believers? (10:100)

---

28. p. 427.
29. Riyadh Edition, II, 281–282.
30. Egyptian Edition, I, 387.
31. III, 12–13.

as authority sanctioning this opinion.

Ibn Kathīr[32] apparently takes a broad view of this verse and remarks that it would serve no useful purpose for a person blind of heart and whose hearing and seeing faculties are sealed by Providence, to enter the fold of Islam, under coercion. He then mentions the *Sha'n al-Nuzūl* to be the case of the Anṣār woman who wanted to retrieve her son from the Jews but adds that the injunction contained in the verse is general in character.

The *Tafsīr al-Manār*[33] describes the commandment contained in this verse as one of the greatest principles of the Islamic faith and one of the majestic pillars of Islamic polity (*siyāsah*). The compiler formulates the principle in these terms: "It is not permissible to subject anyone to coercion to make him accept Islam, nor will anyone be heard to say that a member of his household was compelled to go out from it," and cites the verse: "And if thy Lord had willed, all who are in the earth would have believed together" in corroboration of this position.

It has also been suggested[34] that, though no one can be forced to adopt Islam against his will, yet if he once joins the Islamic community voluntarily, he will not be allowed to leave the sacred fold but will be compelled to recant if he commits apostasy. To the charge of inconsistency of this view with the verse under discussion and other verses of similar import, the reply is made that the inconsistency would vanish if the proselyte is forewarned that once he voluntarily enters the fortress of Islam, he will not be permitted to leave it alive. In the humble opinion of the present writer, no semantic strait-jacket can possibly yield such an implication from the text of this verse.

---

32. H. 'Imād al-Dīn Abū al-Fidā' Ismā'īl ibn Kathīr, *Tafsīr al-Qur'ān al-'Aẓīm*, I, 310.
33. Rashīd Riḍa, *op. cit.*, III, 39.
34. Abul A'la Mawdudi, *op. cit.*, pp. 50–51.

4. And if they argue with thee (O Muḥammad), say: I have surrendered myself completely to Allah and (so have) those who follow me. And say to those who have received the Scripture and those that are unlettered: Have you (also) surrendered? If they surrender, then truly they are rightly guided, and if they turn away, then it is thy duty to convey the message (unto them). And Allah is watchful of (His) bondmen. (3:20)

5. Say: O people of the Scripture! come to an agreement between us and you: that we shall worship none but Allah and that we shall ascribe no partner unto Him and that none of us shall take others for lords besides Allah. And if they turn away, then say: Bear witness that we are they who have surrendered (unto Him). (3:64)

6. He who turns back on his heels shall do no hurt to Allah at all and Allah will reward the thankful. (3:144)

7. Whoso obeys the Messenger obeys Allah and whoso turns away, (then) We have not sent thee as a warder over them. (4:80)

8. And whoso opposeth the Messenger after the guidance (of Allah) has become manifest to him and follows other than the believers' way, We appoint for him that to which he has himself turned and cast him into Hell—a hapless journey's end. (4:115)

9. And if you disbelieve, lo! to Allah belongs whatsoever is in the heavens and whatsoever is in the earth and Allah is Self-Sufficient, Owner of Praise. (4:131)

10. For each of you, We have prescribed a Divine Law and a traced-out way. Had Allah willed He could have made you one community but (He wishes) to try you by that which He has given you. So vie with one another in good works. (5:48)

11. Obey Allah and obey the Messenger and beware! But if you turn away, then know that the duty of Our Messenger is only plain conveyance (of the message). (5:92)

12. The duty of the Messenger is only to convey (the message). Allah knows what you proclaim and what you hide. (5:99)

13. O you who believe! you have charge of your own souls. He who goes astray cannot injure you if you are rightly guided. To Allah

you will all return; and then He will inform you of what you used to do. (5:105)

14. And if their aversion is grievous unto thee, then if thou canst, seek a way down into the earth or a ladder unto heaven that thou mayest bring unto them a portent (to convince them all)! If Allah willed, He could have brought them all together to the guidance—so be not thou among the foolish ones. (6:35)

15. We send not the messengers save as bearers of good and as warrens. So those who believe and do right, no fear shall come upon them, neither shall they grieve. (6:48)

16. Thy people (O Muḥammad) have denied it, though it is the truth. Say: I am not put in charge of you. (6:66)

17. Proofs have come unto you from your Lord, so whoso sees, it is for his own good, and whoso is blind is blind to his own hurt. And I am not a keeper over you. (6:104)

18. Had Allah willed, they would not have set up gods with Him. We have not set thee as a keeper over them, nor art thou responsible for them. (6:107)

19. Thus have We appointed unto every Prophet an adversary—devils of mankind and Jinn, who inspire in one another plausible discourse through guile. If thy Lord willed, they would not do so; so leave them alone with their devising. (6:112)

20. Say: For Allah's is the final argument—had He willed, He could have guided all of you. (6:149)

21. And fight them until persecution is no more and religion is all for Allah. But if they desist, Allah is seer of what they do. (8:39)

22. And if they incline to peace, incline thou also to it and trust in Allah. Lo! He is the Hearer, the Knower. (8:61)

23. And if any one of the idolaters seeks thy protection (O Muḥammad), then protect him so that he may hear the word of Allah and afterwards convey him to his place of safety. That is because they are a folk who know not. (9:6)

24. Know they not that whoso opposes Allah and His Messenger, his portion verily is Hell, to abide therein? That is the extreme abasement. (9:63)

25. And if they deny thee, say: Unto me my work and unto you your work. You are innocent of what I do, and I am innocent of what you do. (10:41)

26. And if thy Lord willed, all who were in the earth would have believed together. Wouldst thou (Muḥammad) compel men until they are believers? (10:99)

27. Say: O mankind! now has the truth come to you from your Lord. So whosoever is guided it is only for (the good of) his own soul and whosoever errs, errs only against it. And I am not a warder over you. (10:108)

28. And if thy Lord had willed, He verily would have made mankind one nation but they would not cease to differ, save him on whom thy Lord has mercy and for that He did create them (11:118–119).

29. And most men will not believe even though thou ardently desire (it). (12:103)

30. Do not those who believe know that, had Allah willed, He could have guided all mankind? (13:31)

31. And Allah's is the direction of way and some (roads) go not straight, and had He willed He would have led you all right. (16: 9)

32. Whosoever follows the right way follows it only for the good of his own soul and whosoever errs, errs only to its hurt. No laden soul can bear another's load. We never punish until We have sent a messenger. (17:15)

33. Say: (It is) the truth from your Lord. Then whosoever will, let him believe and whosoever will, let him disbelieve. Verily We have prepared for the wrongdoers fire whose (flaming) canopy shall enclose them. (18:29)

34. Say: Obey Allah and obey the Messenger. But if you turn away, he is responsible for what he is charged with and you are responsible for what you are charged with. If you obey him, you will go aright. And the Messenger has no other charge than to convey (the message) plainly. (24:54)

35. Nor canst thou lead the blind out of their error. Thou canst make none to hear, save those who believe in Our revelations, so they submit (27:81).

36. And whoso goes right goes right only for (the good) of his own soul; and as for him who goes astray—say: I am only a warner. (27:92)

37. Surely thou canst not guide whomsoever thou lovest; but Allah guides whomsoever He pleases; and He is best aware of those who walk aright. (28:56)

38. For verily thou (Muḥammad) canst not make the dead to hear, nor canst thou make the deaf to hear the call, when they retreat, turning their backs; nor canst thou guide the blind out of their error. Thou canst make none to hear save those who believe in Our revelations so that they submit (to Him). (30:52–53)

39. And as for him who disbelieves, let not his disbelief grieve thee; unto Us is their return and We shall tell them what they did. Lo! Allah is aware of what is in the breasts (of men). (31:23)

40. Is he, the evil of whose deeds is made fair-seeming unto him so that he deemeth it good (like one who believes and does good deeds)? Verily Allah lets go astray whom He wills and guides whom He wills. So let not thy soul expire in sighings for them. Lo! Allah is aware of what they do! (35:8)

41. Say: Allah I worship, making my religion pure for Him (only). Then worship what ye will besides Him. Say: The losers will be those who lose themselves and their house-folk on the Day of Resurrection. (39:14–15)

42. Verily We have revealed to thee the Book for mankind with truth. Then whosoever follows guidance, it is for his own soul and whosoever goes astray, strays only to its hurt. And thou art not a warder over them. (39:41)

43. Lo! those who disbelieve and hinder (man) from the Way of Allah and oppose the Messenger after guidance has become manifest to them, they hurt Allah not a jot, and He will make their actions fruitless. (47:32)

44. We are best aware of what they say, and thou art in no wise a compeller over them. But warn by the Qur'an him who fears My warning. (50:45)

45. Obey Allah and obey His Messenger; but if you turn away, then the duty of Our Messenger is only to convey (the message) plainly. (64:12)

46. So let them chat and play until they meet their Day which they are promised. (70:42)

47. (My responsibility is) only conveyance (of the truth) from Allah and His Messages; and whoso disobeys Allah and His Messenger, surely for him is the Fire of Hell wherein he shall abide. (72:23)

48. Remind them, for thou art but a remembrancer; thou art not at all a warder over them. (88:21–22)

49. Unto you your religion and unto me my religion. (109:6)

These Divine ordinances provide the keynote for the conduct of Muslims in war and peace. The climate of tolerance and human liberty which they signalise would form an illuminating background for a true understanding of the Qur'anic injunctions which bear directly or indirectly on the fate of those for whom the truth is obscured by the workings of their erring minds and who decide to give up their allegiance to Islam for another creed. It is manifest that the Divine Scheme envisaged by the Qur'an gives ample scope for the evolution of the human personality during its earthly existence, in an empirically oriented atmosphere. The Qur'an declares expressly:

> And verily We shall try you till We know those of you who strive hard (for the cause of Allah) and the steadfast *and till We test your record*. And We will make known the (true) facts about you. (47:31)

Guidance for the good life is furnished but not at the cost of suppression of human dignity. Vistas of a future life in which the fruits of action in the present life are to be harvested are also held up before the thinking individual, but the existential choice is left to the individual himself. No reward can be earned by action motivated by coercion—the mind and hand of man must be in harmony if best results of his activity are to be ensured. Islam to be Islam must be accepted absolutely voluntarily by a free person.[35] The Qur'an talks of "the nature (framed) of Allah, in which He has created man" (30:30). The "nature of Allah" is Divine Unity which carries within its concept, by implication, the unity of mankind. This nature, in other words, is Islam and to it the Prophet in a well known saying referred when he said: "Every child is born according to the *fiṭrah* (Nature), and then his parents make him a Jew, a Christian or a Magian" (al-Bukhārī). The religion to which unsullied human nature conforms and instinctively reacts is Islam, but it is his environment and the training he receives under the tutelage of his parents that subsequently fashion his beliefs. After distinguishing the true from the false, God's Book leaves the individual sensibility free choice of direction in the spiritual realm.

Section II—Verses Bearing on Apostasy

The verses in the Qur'an which refer to apostasy and its effects are dispersed throughout the Word of God. We will consider them in the order in which they appear in the Qur'an.

1. And they will not cease from fighting against you till they have made you renegades from your religion, if they can. And whoso from among you turns back from his Faith and dies while he is a disbeliever: such are they whose works shall be vain in this world and in the Hereafter. These are the inmates of the Fire and therein they shall abide. (2:217)

The verse clearly envisages the natural death of the renegade after apostasy. The word used in the Arabic text *fayamūt* is significant. At another place, the Qur'an itself distinguishes between natural death and death by being slain, in the verse:

---

35. Al-Sāmarā'ī, *op. cit.*, pp. 73–74.

"And Muḥammad is but a messenger; messengers (the like of him) have passed away before him. If then he *dies* or is *slain*, will you turn back on your heels?" (3:144). The two words in the original are *māta* and *qutila*. The implication of the verse is unmistakable that the Qur'anic scheme visualises an apostate dying a natural death and there is no hint here that he can be killed for his defection. That the verse is addressed to Muslims is borne out by the expression *minkum* (from among you) and the reference is thus to a Muslim who becomes a renegade. Shaykh Ismā'īl al-Ḥaqqī, in his *Rūḥ al-Bayān*,[36] says in respect of this verse: "This contains a warning against apostasy and in it is inducement to revert to Islam, after apostasy, till the time of death." This commentator, therefore, clearly contemplates the period of repentance to be coterminous with the death of the renegade. Al-Zamakhsharī also interprets the verse[37] in the sense that it imports the death of the renegade in a state of apostasy. The consequences of such apostasy are declared in the verse to be "his deprivation of the fruits of Islam enjoyed by Muslims in this world and falling away of the reward in the Hereafter, due to his continuing in a state of apostasy till death," in the words of al-Zamakhsharī. This view is also shared by al-Ālūsī, al-Baghdādī[38] and other commentators like al-Qāsimī[39] and al-Nīshāpūrī.[40]

There is difference of opinion among commentators as to whether death in the condition of apostasy is necessary to wash away a man's good deeds, performed when he was a Muslim, or whether the incidence of apostasy simpliciter would have that effect, and authorities of Imām al-Shāfi'ī, Imām Abū Ḥanīfah

---

36. 1/2, 335.
37. Al-Sāmarā'ī, *op. cit.*, p. 22.
38. *Ibid.*, 319–326.
39. *Ibid.*
40. *Ibid.*

and Imām Mālik are cited in support of opposing views. A further difference of opinion exists on the question whether the *thawāb* (reward) of his good deeds reverts to him on his return to the true faith subsequently or not. Opinions of Fakhr al-Dīn al-Rāzī, al-Qurṭubī, al-Ṭabarasī and al-Ālūsī are discussed in this context by al-Sāmarā'ī.[41] Al-Ṭabarasī goes to the length of saying that apostasy has the effect of wiping out all actions of the renegade and it is as if those actions had never been, initially. However, al-Nīshāpūrī commits himself to the view that, among other disadvantages incurred by the renegade, he is to be fought against, till overpowered and then killed. For this extreme view apparently no authority is cited. It is pertinent to observe, however, that fighting with an apostate (who is inclined to fight) is quite different from adjudging an apostate liable to the capital sentence, as soon as apostasy occurs. An anonymous writer in the Daily *Zamīndār* of Lahore, dated 15 October 1924, advanced the wholly unacceptable suggestion that the words *ḥabiṭat a'mālahum fī al-dunyā* (their actions in this world become null and void) could be equated on the authority of *Tafsīr Khāzin*[42] with "they [the apostates] are to be wiped off the surface of the earth''. The attempt to shift the consequences of apostasy from actions of the apostate to his person, by a linguistic *tour de force*, must rank as one of the curiosities of polemical literature. The *Tafsīr Khāzin* apparently, only categorises the generally accepted consequences of apostasy, according to orthodox tradition, included among them being the penalty of death, in the comment under the word *ḥabiṭa,* without suggesting an etymological connection between the word and the penalty. Another brave suggestion emanated from an anonymous writer in the *Zamīndār*

41. *Ibid.*
42. *Tafsīr Khāzin*, I, 155.

dated 20 March 1925 that the word *fayamūt* (and he dies) is not inconsistent with other punishments like death being inflicted on him. This must be passed over without comment.

Samuel M. Zwemer, in *The Law of Apostasy in Islam*,[43] categorically asserts that al-Tha'ālibī and al-Rāzī in their commentaries on the Qur'an uphold the view that this verse, "whatever its grammatical construction may be, demands the death of the apostate". I have studied the comments of al-Rāzī in his *Al-Tafsīr al-Kabīr* and those of al-Tha'ālibī in his *Al-Jawāhir al-Ḥisān fī Tafsīr al-Qur'ān* under this verse and find no warrant for the above conclusion. The opinion of Reverend Zwemer is wholly gratuitous and disingenuous. Merely because these exegetes have mentioned in their comments under this verse the usually accepted punishment for apostasy among other disadvantages that the apostate suffers, it does not establish any link between the meaning of the verse and the punishment for apostasy. Change of faith on the part of a Muslim might entail changes in his civil status as to rights of property or marital status, etc., but these incidents follow from other *nuṣūṣ* (clear texts), and additionally from the fact that this *āyah* declares all his actions to be null and void. A discussion of those incidents would lead us beyond the confines of our theme and must be reserved for another occasion. But the suggestion that this verse can be stretched to support the death penalty for apostasy is extremely far fetched.

2. How shall Allah guide a people who disbelieved after their belief and who had borne witness that the Messenger is true and to whom clear proofs had come. And Allah guides not the wrongdoing people.

---

43. S. Zwemer, *The Law of Apostasy in Islam*, pp. 34–35.

As for such, their guerdon is that on them rests the curse of Allah and of angels and of men combined.

They shall abide thereunder. Their doom shall not be lightened, nor shall they be reprieved;

Save those who afterwards repent and do right. Lo! Allah is Forgiving, Merciful.

Surely, those who disbelieve after their (profession of) belief and then increase in disbelief: their repentance will not be accepted. These are they who have gone astray.

As for those who have disbelieved and die while they are disbelievers, the (whole) earth full of gold would not be accepted from any one of them, if it were offered as a ransom (for his soul). Theirs will be a painful doom and they will have no helpers (3:86–91).

Commentators have given varying versions as to the occasion on which these verses were revealed. Ibn Jarīr al-Ṭabarī narrates several such reports in his *Tafsīr Jāmi' al-Bayān*.[44] It is said:

i. Verse 86 was revealed in connection with the case of Ḥārith bin Suwayd al-Anṣārī (or his companion) who had apostatised from Islam but later wanted to revert to the true faith. (This version is also mentioned by al-Qurṭubī in his *Al-Jāmi'*, *vide* al-Sāmarā'ī's *Aḥkām al-Murtadd*[45] where the authority of Ibn 'Abbās is cited for it.)

ii. It was revealed to cover the cases of twelve persons, including Abū 'Āmir the anchorite and the above-mentioned Ḥārth, who became apostates and wanted to return to the fold of Islam.

iii. This verse and verse 89 have reference to those People of the Scripture who had believed in Prophets like Moses, Jesus and others, but, although they had read the prophesies about the Prophet Muḥammad in the Torah and the Bible, they refused to acknowledge him as a true Prophet

---

44. III, 223–224 *et seq.*
45. p. 32.

iv. It may also refer to those Muslims who had become renegades from Islam.

v.   Verse 89 in particular has reference to Jews who knew about the Prophet Muḥammad's advent from their own religious Books but denied him, nevertheless.

In *Al-Baḥr al-Muḥīṭ*, the meaning of the expression *"azdādū kufran"* (increase in disbelief) is assigned the construction, according to one opinion, that they persisted in their disbelief till death and that the verses under consideration cover the Jews as well as Muslim apostates. It is also mentioned therein that some say they were revealed in the case of the companions of Ḥārith bin Suwayd.[46]

Al-Rāzī in his *Al-Tafsīr al-Kabīr*[47] has written comprehensively on the subject of its *Sha'n al-Nuzūl*. According to the various glosses mentioned by him the following possibilities are open:

a. The reference to increase in disbelief in verse 89 is intended to convey the idea that the persons concerned persisted and firmly adhered to their denial of the Prophet with vehement insistence.

b. Over their first disbelief was superadded another disbelief. Under this head there are also variant traditions. One version is that the People of the Book had known of the Prophet's advent, denied him, and then increased in their disbelief, by active opposition to him and by intriguing against him. Another version confines it to Jews who believed in Moses but declined to accept Jesus and his mission, thus becoming disbelievers. They increased their disbelief by rejecting the Qur'an and the Prophet Muḥammad.

---

46. II, 519.
47. II, 491.

c. This was revealed to cover the case of those Muslims who became apostates and moved to Makkah. During their stay in Makkah this disbelief was enhanced by their declaration that they would wait for misfortunes to befall the Prophet.

d. This is intended to refer to persons who had joined the Islamic community as hypocrites and their hypocrisy was described as *kufr* (disbelief) by Allah.

The fact is that the words of the verses are general and would cover the case of Muslims who renounce Islam and then, by insistence on their disbelief, intensify it. As al-Qurṭubī[48] remarks in his *Al-Jāmi'*, various opinions have been given about the subject of these verses but "we conclude from the general nature of the expressions used therein that they are applicable to those Muslims who had defected from Islam and, by insistence on their disbelief, intensified it''.

Al-Ālūsī, in his *Rūḥ al-Ma'ānī*, also affirms this principle of interpretation in these words:

And the occasion for revelation does not reconcile it with particularisation. For the interpretation, as has been settled, is in accordance with the words and not confined to the cause.[49]

Al-Rāzī, too, in *Al-Tafsīr al-Kabīr*, specially mentions this recognised principle of exegesis.[50]

The important thing to note about the contents of these verses is: firstly, that they hold out a promise of God's Grace, if there is genuine repentance on the part of the renegade and that repentance is not limited to any point of time, except that a deathbed repentance would not be acceptable as is expressly declared by the Qur'an elsewhere (see 4:18); secondly, it is

---

48. Al-Sāmarā'ī, *op. cit.*, pp. 29, 30, 32.
49. VI, 118–22, and II, 294.
50. III, 407.

significant that the last of these verses contemplates the natural death of the apostates and there will be awaiting them a painful doom in the Hereafter. There is no suggestion, veiled or otherwise, conveyed by any of these verses that the apostate is to be punished for his disbelief here, during his earthly existence.

3. On the day when (some) faces will be whitened and (some) faces will be blackened; and as for those whose faces will be black, it will be said unto them: Did you disbelieve after believing? Taste then the punishment because of your disbelief. (3:106)

This clearly implies the negation of punishment till the Day of Reckoning in the Hereafter. Qatādah[51] was of the opinion that this verse applies to apostates, on the authority of a tradition narrated by Abū Hurayrah. Al-Qurṭubī also mentions this in his *Al-Jāmi'*.

4. Those who purchase disbelief, at the price of faith, harm Allah not at all but theirs will be a painful doom. (3:177)

Al-Qurṭubī has commented on the authority of Ibn 'Abbās that this applies to those who forsake Islam for disbelief.[52] But no mention is made anywhere of any punishment being inflicted on an apostate, by a mundane tribunal, on the authority of this verse. Indeed the next verse talks of a Divine Plan to allow respite to such people who will increase in disbelief and deserve their doom. That would be a process spread over an undefined period of time.

5. Those who believe, then disbelieve, and then (again) believe, then disbelieve, and then increase in disbelief, Allah will never pardon them, nor will He guide them to the (right) way. (4:137)

This is a striking pronouncement and almost conclusive against the thesis that an apostate must lose his head immediately after his defection from the faith. The verse visualises repeated

---

51. *Ibid.*; al-Sāmarā'ī, *op. cit.,* pp. 29, 30. 32.
52. *Ibid.*

apostasies and reversions to the faith, without mention of any punishment for any of these defections on this earth. The act of apostasy must, therefore, be a sin and not a crime. If he had to be killed for his very first defection, he could not possibly have a history of conversions. This interpretation also found favour with Mawlana Abū al-Wafā' Thanā'ullah of Amritsar, a well-known *Ahl al-Ḥadīth* scholar, *vide* his *Islām aur Masīḥiyyat.*[53] The learned author has discussed this verse therein, in conjunction with the relevant *aḥādīth*.

Al-Sāmarā'ī[54] quotes from al-Qurṭubī the opinion that this verse relates, among others, to *murtaddīn* (apostates). It is also, incidentally, inconsistent with the theory of repentance being admissible for a fixed period of three days or more (which we will discuss later on) for the words *azdādū kufran* (increase in disbelief) introduce an element of indefiniteness as regards any such temporal limitations on the chance to reform. The author of *Rūḥ al-Ma'ānī*[55] traces an opinion to Ḥasan al-Baṣrī that this verse pertains to a group of people from the *Ahl al-Kitāb* (People of the Book) who decided to create doubts about the religion in the minds of the Companions of the Prophet, by professing faith in their presence, then saying that a doubt had afflicted them, again professing faith, and then again proclaiming that another doubt had arisen in their minds and finally persisting in their disbelief till death. History does not record the slaying of any such person for his disbelief, at any stage. Ḥasan thought this episode was also reflected in the verse: "And a party of the People of the Scripture say: Believe in that which has been revealed unto the believers, at the opening of the day and disbelieve at the end thereof in order that they may return" (3:72).

---

53. pp. 202–204.
54. *op. cit.*, p. 30.
55. Al-Ālūsī, *op. cit.*, V, 153–54; II, 196.

But the better opinion seems to be that verse 4:137 is applicable to Muslims who committed apostasy, for the generality of the words occurring therein support this interpretation. Imām al-Rāzī too mentions that most of the scholars have preferred the construction that it is addressed to Muslim renegades.[56]

6. The only reward of those who make war upon Allah and His Messenger and strive to create disorder in the land will be that they will be killed or crucified or have their hands and feet, on alternative sides, cut off or will be expelled out of the land. Such will be their degradation in the land and in the Hereafter; theirs will be an awful doom, save those who repent before you overpower them. For know that Allah is Forgiving, Merciful (5:33–34).

According to Ibn 'Abbās,[57] these verses have relevance to the tribe of Hilāl bin 'Uwaymir, who were polytheists and who had killed and looted members of the Banī Kinānah when the latter had declared their intention to migrate and accept Islam. He explained that the various punishments mentioned in the verses could be inflicted alternatively to suit the nature of the crime—if it was a case of murder unaccompanied by any other crime, the punishment would be death; if in addition there was robbery or dacoity, the delinquents would be crucified, and if it was a case of deprivation of property alone, the cutting off of the right hand and the left foot would be appropriate. In a simple case of intimidation without more, if captured immediately after the crime, the culprits could be imprisoned. If however, before they are overpowered, criminals repent, then God Almighty would be Forgiving and Merciful.

---

56. *Al-Tafsīr al-Kabīr*, III, 330.
57. *Tafsīr*, with al-Suyūṭī, *Lubāb al-Nuqūl fī Asbāb al-Nuzūl* (Urdu translation), I, 264 *et seq*.

Al-Suyūṭī in *Lubāb al-Nuqūl fī Asbāb al-Nuzūl*[58] and al-Ṭabarī in *Jāmi'al-Bayān*[59] mention a report from Anas and another from 'Abd al-Razzāq who traces it from Abū Hurayrah, that these verses were revealed with reference to the people of 'Urīnah, who, when ailing, were sent to live with the flock of camels of the Prophet, under the charge of his grazier. They became renegades, brutally killed the grazier and drove away the camels. They were brought back and subjected to the same treatment as they had meted out to the grazier. M. Muḥammad Shafī', of the Dār al-'Ulūm, Deoband, writing in the Daily *Zamīndar* (Lahore) dated 23 and 24 October 1924,[60] roundly suggested that the verse pertained to persons who became apostates in the Prophet's time and were killed on that account. This is not quite accurate for they had committed the crime of murder with torture and dacoity or robbery as rebels, besides leaving the fold of Islam and the presumption that they were killed for apostasy alone is not consistent with the facts. This incident is also related with all its details in *Ṣaḥīḥ al-Bukhārī*,[61] *Fatḥ al-Bārī*,[62] *'Umdat al-Qārī*[63] and by the author of *Rūḥ al-Ma'ānī*,[64] but the latter prefers the authoritative report (which is endorsed by al-Ṭabarasī and on which practically all *Fuqahā'* are agreed, according to him) that the revelation came to cover the case of highwaymen, robbers and dacoits. He points out that the expression "who make war on Allah and His Messenger" is meant to refer to "people who make war against the Muslims,"

---

58. *Ibid.*

59. pp. 223–224.

60. The Mawlana's article has also been reproduced in his book, *Jawāhir al-Fiqh*, II, 165 *et seq.*

61. Na'ib Naqwi and Muhammad 'Ali, Tr., Arabic-Urdu, III, 555–556.

62. 'Asqalānī, *Fatḥ al-Bārī*, XI, 91–92.

63. Al-'Aynī *'Umdat al-Qārī*, XI, 143.

64. VI, 118–122.

ie., against the community. He also notices differing opinions as to whether the words *yunfūn min al-arḍ*, occurring in the verse, mean "they will be imprisoned" or "they will be banished from the land". Both variants are etymologically possible. He reasons that in the verses it is said that the opportunity for repentance would be gone after they have been overpowered, but in the case of *murtaddīn, tawbah* (repentance) is always possible irrespective of whether they are in the power of the Muslims or not, and consequently he favours the highwaymen version. *Ḥadd* (prescribed punishment), he says, once incurred in Islam, does not lapse. He significantly adds that the ground of revelation does not control the meaning of the verses. Al-Zamakhsharī[65] and al-Bayḍāwī[66] also fall into line with others in accepting the application of the verse to highwaymen, freebooters, etc., *ie.,* active rebels. Al-Rāzī in *Al-Tafsīr al-Kabīr*[67] has recounted all variant opinions under these verses, including those detailed above.

What constitutes *muḥāribah* (making war), as mentioned in these verses, is also a question on which there exists some controversy. It is noteworthy that in the Qur'an itself, the person who inspired the idea of "Masjid Ḍarār," for creating differences and dissensions among the Muslims (he is said to be one, Abū 'Āmir Rāhib) is referred to as one who warred against Allah and His Messenger.[68] The identification of this warring opponent with Abū 'Āmir is mentioned in *Al-Durr al-Manthūr* of al-Suyūṭī,[69] on the authority of Mujāhid. The sinister part played by Abū 'Āmir in this episode is described in the *Baḥr al-Muḥīṭ*,[70] and it is emphasised therein that he was an active enemy of the

---

65. *op. cit.,* I, 227 *et seq.*
66. *Tafsīr* on the margin of *Al-Qur'ān al-Ḥakīm* (Egypt), p. 114.
67. III, 407.
68. 9:107.
69. III, 276.
70. V, 98.

Muslims, who had promised to bring soldiers from Rome to fight them. In another part of the same book[71] the dictum of Ibn 'Abbās that *muḥāribah* is *shirk* (polytheism) and that of 'Urwah that it is equated with *irtidād* (apostasy) are contested and characterised as *ghayr ṣaḥīḥ 'ind al-jamhūr*—not correct according to the majority of the doctors. The above-mentioned writer in the *Zamīndār* has relied upon a saying of Sa'īd bin Jābir that *muḥāribah* means disbelief and has further cited the opinion of Ibn Baṭal from *Fatḥ al-Bārī*[72] (which is a commentary on the *Ṣaḥīḥ al-Bukhārī*) in its support. Al-'Aynī[73] too ascribes an opinion to al-Bukhārī that by *yuḥāribūn Allāh* is meant disbelievers. Al-'Aynī himself apparently, while commenting on the dictum in the *Hidāyah* that an apostate is a *ḥarbī* (fighter),[74] says that this classification is correct as he is neither a *dhimmī* nor a *mustā'min*. This process of elimination ignores the fact that there can be a third category of disbelievers—*mu'āhids*—people with whom there is a pact of mutual defence. But al-Bayḍāwī and al-Ālūsī give the root meaning of *ḥarb* as *al-salb* or *al-salab wa al-akhdh*, ie., forcible deprivation or seizure of property. Etymologically, therefore, the equation of *muḥāribah* with disbelief or apostasy has not much to commend itself. Its identification with these two phenomena probably has its genesis in an insufficient appreciation of relevant historical facts. In this context, it may be useful to remember the Divine injunction: "Whosoever kills a human being for other than manslaughter or corruption in the earth, it shall be as if he had killed all mankind" (5:32).

---

71. III, 470–471.
72. XI, 91–92.
73. *op. cit.*, XI, 143–144.
74. *Ibid.*

Muslim scholars in recent times have expressly declared that disbelief by itself does not justify killing of the disbeliever but that there must be superadded thereto an element of either war against Muslims or enmity against them or creation of circumstances which make their profession of the faith a trial for them, to justify such action. Shaykh Maḥmūd Shaltūt has forcefully expressed himself on this point in his book *Al-Islām, 'Aqīdah wa Sharī'ah.*[75] He has also reiterated his opinion in connection with the interpretation of the verse: "And end not the life that Allah has made sacred, save in the course of justice" (6:151), in his *Tafsīr.*[76] Al-Sāmarā'ī[77] has marshalled other authorities in support of this position—notably those of Ibn Daqīq cited from his *Iḥkām al-Aḥkām Sharḥ 'Umdat al-Iḥkām* (quoted from his *Fī al-'Iddah 'alā al-Iḥkām al-Aḥkām*).

The Aḥnāf and the Imāmiyyah, in contrast with other schools of thought, further differentiate between male and female apostates and hold that female apostates are not to be killed but only imprisoned, on the ground that they are not capable of fighting actively. The subject will be found discussed adequately by al-Sāmarā'ī[78] in *Aḥkām al-Murtadd*, wherein the relevant authorities are cited. Reference in this connection may also be made to *Al-Mughnī*[79] by Ibn Qudāmah, *Muqaddamah*[80] by Ibn Rushd, *Fatḥ al-Bārī,*[81] *'Umdat al-Qārī,*[82] *Fatḥ al-Qadīr,*[83]

---

75. pp. 300–01.

76. *Tafsīr al-Qur'ān al-Ḥakīm*, p. 427.

77. *op. cit.*, pp. 115–116.

78. *Ibid.*, pp. 213 *et seq.*

79. VIII, 123.

80. I, 371.

81. XII, 228 *et seq.*

82. XI. 232–239.

83. *Sharḥ Fatḥ al-Qadīr 'alā Hidāyat Sharḥ Bidāyah* and on its margin, *Sharḥ 'Ināyah 'alā al-Hidāyah* with commentary by al-Chalpī on *Fatḥ al-Qadīr*, IV, 388–389.

Hidāyah,[84] and *'Ināyah*,[85] wherein instances of the Prophet forbidding the killing of women for their lack of fighting capacity are mentioned and the view is upheld that the slaying of a person is grounded on *ḥirāb* (fighting or active enmity) and not merely on change of faith. In the early years of Islam, the fact that persons who defected from the religion also joined the enemy groups may have obscured the distinction between peaceful renegades and apostates who actively opposed the faithful. Al-Chalpī,[86] in his comments on *Fatḥ al-Qadīr*, cites Ibn Hammām's opinion that "there is no punishment for the act of apostasy, for its punishment is greater than that, with God". This is an extremely significant comment, in harmony with the letter and spirit of the Qur'anic text. But, strangely enough, these learned commentators, despite these rational dicta, stick to the traditional view that an apostate must be killed when they deal directly with the problem of apostasy. They appear to be supremely unconscious of the inherent contradiction between the two positions.

7. O ye who believe! whoso of you becomes a renegade from his religion, (know that in his stead) Allah will bring a people whom He loves and who love Him, humble towards believers, stern towards disbelievers, striving in the way of Allah, and fearing not the blame of any blamer. Such is the grace of Allah, which He gives unto whom He will. Allah is All-Embracing, All-Knowing (5:54).

Al-Sāmarā'ī[87] has collected opinions of exegetists like al-Ṭabarī, al-Nīshāpūrī, al-Qurṭubī, al-Zamakhsharī, al-Rāzī, and al-Ṭabarasī, on the interpretation of this verse. Their opinions may

---

84. *Ibid.*
85. *Ibid.*
86. *Ibid.*
87. *op. cit.*, pp. 23–28.

be summed up by saying that the verse embodies a warning and a prophecy. The warning conveyed was that apostasy would not affect Divine purposes in the least. The prophecy foreshadowed the apostasy of several tribes on the death of the Prophet and gave the glad tidings that they would be replaced by God-loving and God-loved, true Muslims. The main inference derivable from the verse is that there is no punishment for apostasy to be enforced in this world, for such human aberrations cannot frustrate God's purposes.

8.   Whoso disbelieves in Allah after he has believed—save him who is forced thereto and whose heart is still content with faith—but such as open their breasts to disbelief: on them is wrath from Allah. Theirs will be an awful doom (16:106).

The only punishment mentioned for apostasy in this verse is postponed to the Hereafter. Al-Sāmarā'ī,[88] in his comment on this verse has quoted from al-Qurṭubī's *Al-Jāmi'* the remark that the verse conveys an admonition that the wrath of Allah will be incurred by the apostate, but there is no hint of any other punishment. Dr Samuel M. Zwemer's[89] conjecture that commentators derive justification for the death penalty from this verse read with verse 218, Al-Baqarah, is fanciful. The mere fact that in the *Tafsīr Khāzin*, the various disabilities (including the death sentence) to which an apostate is subject according to the orthodox view, are categorised under verse 218 of Al-Baqarah, cannot support this view, as Dr Zwemer seems to imagine.

9.   And among mankind is he who worships Allah on a narrow marge. Then if good befalls him, he is content therewith, but if a trial befalls him, he returns to his (former) way. He loses both this world and the Hereafter. That is a manifest loss (22:11).

---

88. *Ibid.*, pp. 30–31.
89. *op. cit.*, pp. 34–35.

Al-Qurṭubī,[90] in his *Al-Jāmi'*, records that according to some exegetists this verse was revealed with reference to some Arabs who had accepted Islam and adhered to the faith as long as they enjoyed ease and comfort, but as soon as they encountered hardship, they became renegades. Another report links it with the case of Naḍr bin al-Ḥārith and still another connects it with that of Shaybah bin Rabī'ah who apostatised in circumstances similar to those mentioned above. There is no historical evidence forthcoming that any such person or persons were executed for their defection from the faith.

10. Those who disbelieve and hinder (men) from the way of Allah and oppose the Messenger, after the guidance has become manifest to them, hurt Allah not a jot, and He will make their actions fruitless (47:32).

Al-Sāmarā'ī[91] observes that this verse may possibly be in respect of disbelievers or may concern hypocrites as the context shows that both possibilities are open. Sūrah Muḥammad of the Qur'an starts with a declaration that Allah renders the actions of disbelievers and of those who oppose Allah vain. In the 5th verse of the Sūrah, Muslims are enjoined to fight the disbelievers vigorously when they meet them in regular battle, till such time as "the war lays down its burdens". This means that war is permitted only to ensure peace and not for aggression.

11. O Prophet! Strive hard against the disbelievers and the hypocrites, and be stern with them. Their resort is Hell, a hapless journey's end (66:9).

These words are identical with those of Sūrah al-Tawbah (verse 73). The text by no means justifies the killing of a *murtadd* (apostate) or a *munāfiq* (hypocrite), wantonly, unless

---

90. *vide* al-Sāmarā'ī, *op. cit.*, p. 31.
91. *Ibid.*, p. 33.

there is resort to war on their part. The word *jāhid* occurring in these two verses does not necessarily mean "taking up arms". An earnest effort would be as much within the scope of its connotations as war. In the *Fath al-Bayān*[92] we have the following comment on these words:

> Al-Ṭabarī has said: The opinion to be given preference, according to me, is that contained in the statement of Ibn Masʿūd that *jihād* means the exercise of vigorous effort. The *āyah* implies that *jihād* against the hypocrites is sanctioned but there is no specification of its nature in the verse. It is, therefore, necessary to resort to other guidance. Detailed reasoning has established that *jihād* against disbelievers is to be with the sword and against the hypocrites by adducing of arguments against them at one time, abandoning kindness towards them at another time and sacrifice on another occasion, and this is what Ibn Masʿūd says.

The treatment of hypocrites constitutes a very instructive chapter of Islamic polity. That the character of their professed belief and their identity was known is patent from several verses of the Qur'an. A study of the following, among others, would be rewarding, in this context:

a. And of mankind are some who say: We believe in Allah and the Last Day, when they believe not (2:8).
b. And when they fall in with those who believe, they say: We believe, but when they go apart with their devils (ringleaders) they declare: Lo! we are with you; verily we did but mock. Allah Himself doth mock them, leaving them to wander blindly on, in their contumacy (2:14–15).
c. And when they fall in with those who believe, they say: We believe. But when they meet one another in private, they say: Prate ye to them of that which Allah hath disclosed to you that they may contend with you before your Lord concerning it. Have ye then no

---

92. IV, 134.

sense? Are they then unaware that Allah knoweth that which they keep hidden and that which they proclaim? (2:76–77).

d. And a party of the People of the Scripture say: Declare your belief (outwardly) in that which has been revealed to the believers in the early part of the day and disbelieve in the latter part thereof; perchance they may return (3:72).

The person described in these verses were well known, according to several commentators of the Qur'an. Reference in this connection may be made to *Al-Bahr al-Muhīt,*[93] *Rūh al-Ma'ānī,*[94] *Al-Durr al-Manthūr,*[95] and *Fath al-Bayān,*[96] among others. The first two cite reports that the verses have relevance to twelve leaders of the Jews of Khaybar and of 'Uraynah or that relate to Ka'b bin Ashraf, the Jew, and his companions. The *Bahr al-Muhīt* in its alternative version[97] says that the Jews resented the change of *Qiblah* (the direction in which Muslims face during prayer) from Bayt al-Maqdis to the Ka'bah, and Ka'b bin Ashraf and his companions said: Pray in the same direction as they do in the morning and revert to the direction of the Dome of the Rock in the latter part of the day. These verses were then revealed. Verse 143 of Sūrah al-Baqarah lends indirect support to this interpretation with the words:

> And We appointed the *Qiblah* which thou wouldst have as the *Qiblah* only that We might know him who followeth the Messenger, from him who turneth on his heels.

In either case the identity of the people in question was not in doubt and we have it from the author of *Al-Bahr al-Muhīt* that this conspiracy was actually acted upon. Ibn Jarīr al-Ṭabarī has

---

93. II, 493.
94. III, 199–200.
95. II, 42–43 (quoted by M. Sher 'Ali).
96. II, 60 (quoted by M. Sher 'Ali).
97. II, 493.

also mentioned that some Muslims had committed apostasy on that occasion.[98] As has been noticed earlier, Ḥasan al-Baṣrī has also talked of a similar hypocritical group in the context of Sūrah al-Nisā' (verse 137). The existence of these hypocrites continued to be tolerated within the body politic of Islam without physical interference with them.

e.   What aileth you that you are become two parties regarding the hypocrites? And Allah has cast them back (to disbelief) because of what they earned. Seek ye to guide him whom Allah hath sent astray? He whom Allah sendeth astray, for him thou (O Muḥammad) canst not find a road.

They long that you should disbelieve even as they disbelieve, that you may be upon a level (with them). So choose not friends from them till they emigrate in the way of Allah; if they turn back (to enmity), then take them and kill them wherever ye find them, and choose no friend nor helper from among them; except those who seek refuge with a people between whom and you there is a covenant, or (those who) come unto you because their hearts forbid them to make war on you or make war on their own folk. Had Allah willed He could have given them power over you so that assuredly they would have fought you. So if they hold aloof from you and wage not war against you and offer you peace, Allah allows you no war against them.

You will find others who desire that they should have security from you and security from their own folk. So often as they are returned to hostility they fall headlong into it. If they keep not aloof from you nor offer you peace nor hold their hands, then take them and kill them wherever you find them. Against these We have given you clear authority (4:88–91).

It is plain that even these verses do not permit aggression against hypocrites. If they are peaceful, no action can be taken against them. It is only if they adopt open hostility that they are

---

98. *Tafsīr*, II, 8.

to be engaged in combat and killed. Only an unfair critic, like Dr Zwemer, could have suggested, as he does, by quoting only a part of verses 89 and 90 that they furnish proof of lack of toleration and absence of personal liberty in Muslim Law.[99] Apparently Majid Khadduri[100] sees in verse 89 authority for the death penalty in a case of apostasy—an impossible position in the whole context:

f. Lo! Allah will gather hypocrites and disbelievers, all together into Hell (4:140).

g. Lo! the hypocrites (will be) in the lowest deep of the fire and thou shall find no helper for them (4:145).

These two verses place the hypocrites on a lower level than unbelievers or at least equate them in respect of tortures in the Hereafter. It is not, therefore, that for the hypocrites there is a soft corner in the Qur'anic scheme and, because of it, their peaceful aberrations are to be ignored. The guiding principle is clearly the necessity of a free choice in matters of conscience. Because of their hypocrisy, however, the Prophet is directed to tell them that they will not be permitted to participate in *jihād*, in the company of Muslims (9:83). In verse 54 of Sūrah al-Tawbah they are described as those "who disbelieve in Allah and His Messenger". In verse 56 of that Sūrah, it is clarified that, despite their oaths to the contrary, "they are not of you" and, in verse 84, the Prophet is forbidden to pray for any one of them if he dies, or to stand by his grave, "for they disbelieved in Allah and His Messenger and died while they were disobedient". So they are to be denied the blessings of the Prophet's prayer for them, but otherwise they are left to die their natural death. Their delinquency is such that the Prophet is told (verse 80) that even if forgiveness is asked for them seventy times, they will not be

---

99. *op. cit.*, pp. 33–34.
100. *op. cit.*, pp. 149-152.

pardoned by Allah as they were disbelievers. That their position is not different from that of *murtaddīn* is borne out by verse 74 of that Sūrah—"They swear by Allah that they said nothing (wrong), yet they did utter the word of disbelief and disbelieved after their (acceptance of) Islam and they purposed that which they could not attain and they cherished enmity (against believers) only that Allah by His Messenger should enrich them of His bounty." Ibn Hishām[101] records in his *Life of the Prophet* that this verse was revealed in respect of Julās bin Suwayd bin Ṣāmit who did not accompany the Prophet for the expedition to Tabūk, and made a disparaging remark about the Prophet. When taxed with it, he denied on oath that he had said anything. Apparently no punishment was awarded to him. Other hypocrites are specifically named by Ibn Hishām and he even links their cases with certain verses of the Qur'an. They all remained free from punishment. In verse 66 also, it is proclaimed that they disbelieved after having believed. The opening verses of Sūrah al-Munāfiqīn declare that the hypocrites' proclamation of faith is false and "they have made their oaths a cloak, thus to hinder (men) from the path of Allah". In the third verse of that Sūrah, it is clearly stated that they first believed and then disbelieved. But no one smote their neck on that account.

Indirect support is also provided for freedom of conscience in the Divine Scheme by various recitals in the Qur'an to the effect that it was the disbelievers in the communities to which various Prophets were sent, who threatened to banish the Messenger of God from their lands, unless they reverted to their faith. Instances in point are of the people of Shu'ayb (7:88) and of the Pharaoh threatening sorcerers with torture for daring to believe in "the Lord of Moses and Aaron", without asking for his

---

101. *Sīrah*, Urdu translation by M. Qutb al-Din Ahmad Mahmudi, II, 203–205.

permission (26:49). It is stated generally in verse 13 of Sūrah Ibrāhīm: "And those who disbelieved said to their Messengers: We will surely expel you from our land, unless you return to our religion. Then their Lord sent unto them the revelation: We will surely destroy the wrong-doers." Such coercion or persecution could not, therefore, be commendable in the eye of God. The chief of the hypocrites in the Prophet's own time was 'Abdullah bin Ubayy bin Salūl, and history has recorded that he was not killed despite permission to do so being asked of the Prophet by no less a person than 'Abdullah's own son, who was a good Muslim.[102] He had by his perfidious conduct given offence to Muslims on several occasions, but his life was spared.

Some scholars[103] have argued on the basis of verse 54 of Sūrah al-Baqarah that the punishment of death was inflicted on the Israelites for apostasy on account of their calf-worship and that the rule holds good for Muslims also. The verse reads as under:

> And when Moses said to his people: O my people, you have surely wronged yourselves by your choosing the calf (for worship), so turn in penitence to your Creator and kill (the guilty) yourselves. That will be best for you with your Creator and He will relent toward you. Lo! He is the Relenting, the Merciful.

There are some peculiar features of this incident as narrated in the Qur'an. In the first place the erring Israelites had expressed penitence before they were ordered to slay one another. In the second place, it is curious that the principal culprit, Sāmirī, who fashioned the calf and persuaded them to worship it, was himself spared, to die as an ostracised person, later. Apparently Mawlana Shabbir Ahmad 'Uthmani was of the view that Sāmirī was a

---

102. *Ibid.*
103. Mawlana Shabbir Ahmad 'Uthmani in *Risālat al-Shihāb*, as quoted in *Payghām-i Ṣulḥ*, Lahore, for 4 February 1925, and Mawlana Mawdudi in his article published in *Nawā'-i Waqt*, Lahore, dated 28 July 1973.

hypocrite and not an apostate who worshipped the idol. This is to lose sight of what is said to Sāmirī in verses 97–98 of Sūrah Ṭā Hā about the calf being "thy God of which thou hast remained a votary". In the face of these facts can it be urged with any solemnity that death was imposed as a sentence for their apostasy?

Indeed the story of slaying is itself doubted by some commentators like the author of *Rūḥ al-Bayān*[104] and Abī Ḥayyān, the author of *Al-Baḥr al-Muḥīṭ*[105]. They favoured the interpretation of the Qur'anic word *"faqtulū anfusukum"* as "Kill your base desires," and al-Ālūsī says, in his *Rūḥ al-Ma'ānī*, that he was himself inclined towards this construction but for the pressure of certain reports to the contrary. Incidentally, the Biblical account of the incident in *Exodus* differs materially from the Qur'anic narrative and cannot be implicitly relied upon for details of the alleged collective self-slaughter. Abī Ḥayyān and Ismā'īl Ḥaqqī both clarify that the incident furnishes no binding precedent for the Muslim nation. The former says that, through the mercy of God, desisting from the offence and genuine repentance are enough expiation for a Muslim, and the latter suggests the abrogation of the Israeli rule ''out of respect for the Prophet (on him be peace)''. Older authorities, therefore, do not support the view of Mawlana 'Uthmani and Mawlana Mawdudi on this point.

The position that emerges, after a survey of the relevant verses of the Qur'an, may be summed up by saying that not only is there no punishment for apostasy provided in the Book but that the Word of God clearly envisages the natural death of the apostate without any indication that he can be killed for apostasy. He will be punished only in the Hereafter. The Qur'an also

---

104. I, 93–95.
105. I, 208–209.

visualises the possibility of repeated apostasies by a person, thus negativing the justification or necessity of enforcing the punishment of death on a person who declines to revert to Islam within a limited time, on his very first lapse. Abī Ḥayyān, the well-known exegetist, has expressly mentioned a definite opinion that no apostate can be forced into rejoining the Muslim community. In fact, apostasy is treated as a sin, albeit a very grave sin, and not as a crime by the Qur'an, but the time for repentance is extended, in God's infinite Mercy, to a lifetime short of the actual death agony. For God's purposes cannot be defeated by defections from the Faith of puny mortals, and so the Prophet is enjoined not to worry his soul out, in grief, for those who turn away. He is forbidden to force them to the straight path, for this would interfere with the Divine Scheme of life here being a trial for the human soul. It is repeatedly emphasised that his function is to convey the Message fully and leave the rest to God. The *Dīn* is to be established by goodly exhortation and not by threat of force. The Qur'an itself places hypocrites on a par with apostates but, in their case, history bears out a most humane and liberal policy of tolerance on the part of the Prophet. Violence is permitted to Muslims only against those who fight them or persecute them or spread disorder in the land, and mere change of faith, provided the conversion is peaceful, is not actionable at all in this phenomenal world. An essential element for force being permitted against a person is active hostility on his part and that is why some schools of thought among Muslims exempt women (who from their very nature are presumed to be incapable of bearing arms) and others who may be regarded as disabled, from the punishment for apostasy. The Qur'an includes a unique charter of liberty of conscience for mankind.

CHAPTER II

Apostasy and the Sunnah

Section I

Before taking up the specific *aḥādīth* (traditions) which are relied upon by the proponents of the death sentence for apostasy, it would be useful to clear the ground by a few observations concerning the relative positions of the Qur'an and the Ḥadīth. Imām al-Shāfiʿī in his *Al-Risālah*[1] has clearly enunciated the principle that the commandments contained in the Qur'an can be abrogated only by another verse of the Qur'an and by any authority lower in status. He holds definitely that the *Sunnah* of the Prophet cannot perform any such abrogating function *vis-à-vis* the Qur'an, for it is itself subject to the Book of God in respect of all clear and well-defined Qur'anic texts (*nuṣūṣ*). Of course, he says, it can interpret, explain or expound, with subsidiary details, the summary commandments included in the Qur'an. In support of his position, al-Shāfiʿī cites the verse of the Qur'an:

> And when Our Clear revelations are recited unto them, they who look not for the meeting with Us, say: Bring a Qur'an other than this or change it. Say (O Muḥammad): It is not for me to change it of my own accord. I only follow that which is revealed to me. Lo! if I disobey my Lord, I fear the retribution of an awful day. (10:15)

---

1. Urdu translation by M. Amjad ʿAli, pp. 97 *et seq*.

He also draws strength for his argument from verse 106 of
Sūrah al-Baqarah:

> Whatever revelation We abrogate or cause to be forgotten, We
> bring (in its place) one better or the like thereof. Knowest thou not
> Allah is able to do all things?

Imām Abū Ḥanīfah's dictum is quoted by Mawlana Shibli in
his *Sīrat-i Nu'mān*:

> Nothing that is not proved by *tawātur* (continued tradition) is part
> of the Qur'an and whatever is redundant is abrogated. No addition
> to the Qur'an is permissible simply on the basis of a single-person
> report.[2]

It is thus Allah alone Who can change what has emanated
from Him and, considering the fundamental position of
the Qur'an in Islam, this stands to reason.

Mawlana Badr-i 'Alam Nadvi in his *Tarjumān al-Sunnah*[3]
says, on the authority of extracts from Imām al-Shāṭibī's *Al-
Muwāfaqāt*, that the *Sunnah* occupies a place of secondary
importance as compared with the Book of God and that generally
it can be asserted firmly that the *Sunnah* cannot be placed on the
same level with the Qur'an in point of regard and reverence. This
is the reason why 'Ubaydullah and al-Taftazānī in *Al-Tawḍīḥ wa
al-Talwīḥ*[4] lay it down as a guiding principle that in case of
conflict with the text of the Qur'an, *al-khabar al-waḥīd* (a
tradition related by one person or by a group from one person, so
long as the number of narrators is less than those in the case of
ḥadīth mashhūr [reputed tradition]) will be rejected. It is
explained therein that matters of faith cannot be established by a
solitary *khabar*. Again, al-Taftazānī in his Gloss on the *Tawḍīḥ,*

---

2. *Imām Abū Ḥanīfah, Life and Work* (Eng. trans. of *Sīrat al-Nu'mān,* by M.
Hadi Hussain), p. 176.
3. I, 118 *et seq.*
4. pp. 229–231.

called the *Talwīḥ*, quotes a saying of the Prophet (on him be peace) in these words:

> After me there will be for you multiplicity of *aḥādīth*. If then a *ḥadīth* is related from me, compare it with the Book of God. What accords with it accept and reject whatever contradicts it.

This *ḥadīth* leads to the conclusion that all sayings contradictory to the Book of God are not the Prophet's Ḥadīth (on him be peace) and they are verily forged. Such *ḥadīth* is said to be only *mufīd al-ḍann* (as raising only a presumption). It can neither abrogate the Book nor add to it.

In the fourth chapter of *Ḥujjat Allāh al-Bālighah*,[5] Part I, Shah Waliyullah has categorised the extant compilations of Traditions in their order of reliability and importance. He thinks that only *Al-Muwaṭṭa'* of Imām Mālik, *Ṣaḥīḥ al-Bukhārī* and *Ṣaḥīḥ Muslim* deserve to be placed in the first category. The compilations like those of Abū Dāwūd, al-Tirmidhī, Ibn Mājah and al-Nasā'ī, which are generally included among the *Ṣiḥāḥ al-Sittah* (the Six Accurate Books) and the *Musnad* of Imām Aḥmad, he assigns to the second category. He adds that the *Muḥaddithīn* (Experts in Tradition) consider these two categories only to be worthy of reliance and not the books falling in the third and fourth categories such as the *Musnad* of Abī 'Alī, *Al-Muṣannaf* of 'Abd al-Razzāq, *Al-Muṣannaf* of Abī Bakr bin Abī Shaybah, the *Musnad* of 'Abd bin Ḥamīd, *Musnad* of al-Ṭayālisī, and books by al-Bayhaqī, al-Ṭaḥāwī, al-Ṭabarānī, Ibn Ḥabbān, Ibn 'Adī, al-Khaṭīb, Abī Nu'mān, Ibn 'Asākir, al-Khawārizmī, Ibn al-Najjār, al-Daylamī, and others. There are also fabricated *aḥādīth*, collected and criticised by Mullā 'Alī al-Qāri and Ibn al-Jawzī among others. Traditions themselves are differentiated *inter see* in order of authenticity and reliability. In point of

---

5. Urdu translation by M. 'Abd al-Rahim, I, 619–628.

priority they are designated as *mutawātir* (continuous), *mustafīḍ* (narrated in several ways and accepted), *mashhūr* (reputed), *ṣaḥīh* (accepted as correct) and *ḥasan* (approved), and the lowest tier in this hierarchy is that of *khabar aḥād*. The number and reliability of the chain of narrators, its continuity or otherwise, evidence of implementation or rejection, conformity with the Qur'anic letter or spirit as well as with known historical or rational facts, are some of the factors which determine this order of priority. The human factor of lapse of memory or of failure to comprehend fully the circumstances surrounding a tradition is also a pertinent consideration. The classical instance of 'Ā'ishah's,[6] the Prophet's wife, correcting Ibn 'Umar (or, according to one version, 'Umar, the Second Caliph, himself) in respect of his opinion that the lamentations of a deceased person's relatives entail torture in the after-life for the dead person, is very apt in this context. 'Ā'ishah's comment was that the *ḥadīth* had not been properly understood or recollected. She explained that in fact the Prophet passed by a Jewish woman who had died, and had seen her relatives lamenting, when he observed: "They are crying and she is being subjected to torture." It was wrongly assumed that there was a casual nexus between the two sentences uttered by the Prophet, and she cited the Qur'an: "No bearer of burden can bear the burden of another" (6:164). She evidently invoked the principle that a *ḥadīth* could not be possibly contradict a clear text of the Qur'an and interpreted the reported tradition in its light. Shah Waliyullah too in his *'Iqd al-Jīd* lays down the principle that *Sunnah* only explains the Qur'an and can never contradict it.[7]

---

6. *Ibid.*, I, 655, and M. Sher Ali, *Qatli Murtadd aur Islām*, pp. 100–101. Also Ra'īs Aḥmad Ja'farī, *Talkhīṣ al-Bukhārī*, p. 135, and Na'ib Husain Naqwi, *Mishkāt al-Maṣābīḥ*, I, 394.
7. Quoted in *Fikr-o Naẓar*, September 1971, p. 195.

Imām Abū Yūsuf had warned against solitary *aḥādīth* in these words:

> *Ḥadīth* multiplies so much that some *aḥādīth* which are traced back through chains of transmission are not well known to legal experts nor do they conform to the Qur'an and the *Sunnah*. Beware of solitary *aḥādīth* and keep close to the collective spirit (*al-jamā'ah*) of *Ḥadīth* ... Therefore make the Qur'an and the well-known *Sunnah* your guide and follow it.[8]

Section II

The principal *ḥadīth* on which the case for the death sentence for apostasy is built up is the one narrated by Ibn 'Abbās in the words: "Whosoever changes his religion, slay him." This is given by al-Bukhārī in his *Ṣaḥīḥ*—"*Kitāb al-Jihād fī Istitābat al-Murtaddīn*". To it is annexed the story of 'Alī burning to death a number of *zanādiqah* (heretics), and Ibn 'Abbās, on being informed of the incident, is stated to have remarked that he would not have burnt them but merely killed them, for the Prophet had forbidden the burning of human beings. He then recited this *ḥadīth*.

The same *ḥadīth* is also traced[9] to 'Ā'ishah by al-Ṭabarānī in his *Al-Mu'jam al-Wasṭ*. According to another narrator, Mu'āwiyah bin Hīdah, as recorded in al-Ṭabarānī's *Al-Mu'jam al-Kabīr*, the full *ḥadīth* should read: "Whosever changes his faith, slay him. Verily Allah does not accept repentance from His servant who has adopted disbelief alter having accepted Islam." The latter part of this version apparently contradicts the Qur'anic texts, which we have already noticed, and is unreliable.

---

8. *Al-Radd 'alā Siyar Al-Awzā'ī*, pp. 39–41.
9. Al-Zayla'ī, *Naṣb al-Rāyah li Aḥādīth al-Hidāyah,* Vol. III, Chapter "*Aḥkām al-Murtaddīn*".

Al-Sāmarā'ī[10] reproduces this *ḥadīth* from *Sunan al-Nasā'ī* (*Sharḥ al-Suyūṭī*) and observes that many jurisconsults have accepted its authority, but there is a good deal of difference between them as to its meaning. Imām al-Shāfi'ī and Ibn Ḥazm are reported to have expressed the view that the words of the *ḥadīth* being general, it would apply even to a disbeliever who changes his faith. On the contrary, the majority of the jurisconsults and Imām Mālik held the opinion that it is confined to Muslims who become renegades from Islam. It is pointed out that the logical result of the first view would lead to the absurd proposition that even a disbeliever who adopts Islam ought to be killed for his change of faith. Consequently the *ḥadīth*, according to better opinion, cannot be interpreted in its literal sense and is susceptible of an obvious limitation to Muslims. It is also argued in favour of the second group that, according to another *ḥadīth*, all disbelievers, whatever variety of faiths they may profess, constitute a single community (*millah wāḥidah*) and consequently change from one form of disbelief to another would not alter their position *vis-à-vis* Islam and could not be regarded as a change of faith, in the real sense.

None of these sources, however, indicates the circumstances which provided the occasion for this *qawlī* (verbal) *ḥadīth*. On the face of it, the *ḥadīth* is *mujmal*—a summary statement—and calls for further elucidation. It was because of its *mujmal* character that the late Mawlana Muhammad 'Ali Jawhar expressed the opinion in his article reproduced in the *Payghām-i Ṣulḥ*, Lahore, dated 11 March 1925, that it cannot form the foundation of any *Sharī'ah* law, specially when it runs against the tenor of Qur'anic injunctions. He also drew attention to the fact that one of the narrators of this *ḥadīth* is Abū al-Nu'mān

---

10. *Aḥkām al-Murtadd*, pp. 36–39.

Muḥammad bin al-Faḍl who, according to Ibn Ḥabbān, had become mentally confused in his old age and altered words so that he did not know what he was talking about and lots of unacceptable things crept into his *aḥādīth* requiring their rejection, as stated in the *Tahdhīb al-Tahdhīb*. M. Aslam Jairajpuri suggested that this *mujmal ḥadīth* has to be used with other *aḥādīth* to arrive at its correct connotation and concluded that it applied to persons who left the community to join the active ranks of the enemy, *vide* his article reproduced in the *Payghām-i Ṣulh*, Lahore, dated 23 November 1924.

Difference of opinion prevails among Doctors of Law as to whether it applies to a woman apostate or not. Al-Sāmarā'ī[11] mentions that Imām Mālik, al-Awzā'ī, Imām al-Shāfi'ī and Layth bin Sa'd accepted this *ḥadīth* as sufficient authority for killing a Muslim woman who leaves the fold of Islam, having regard to the general nature of the expressions used therein. However, al-Thawrī, Imam Abū Ḥanīfah and his followers, Ibn Shabramah, Ibn 'Alīyyah, 'Aṭā' and Ḥasan excluded women from its scope. Their argument was that Ibn 'Abbās, the principal narrator of the *ḥadīth*, had himself declared that a female apostate should not be killed,[12] as the Prophet had forbidden the slaying of women in wars. The Shāfi'īs, the Ḥanbalīs, the Zaydīs and the Mālikīs place men and women on the same footing in this respect, but the Ḥanafīs and the Imāmiyyah Shī'ahs say that the woman will be imprisoned till she repents. Al-Sarakhsī, among the *Aḥnāf*, apparently took the view that a woman who was possessed of sound judgement and capacity to give orders can also be condemned to death for apostasy, though, normally, she would be immune from that sentence. Further, al-Sarakhsī makes

---

11. *Ibid.,* pp. 211–222.
12. *Ibid.*

it clear that the *ḥadīth* in question cannot be applicable in its literal sense and because of the Prophet's saying, has to be particularised and confined to Muslim men only. Al-Sāmarā'ī has dealt with the question at length, in *Aḥkām al-Murtadd*. Other authorities too have pointedly referred to this exemption.[13] Imām Muḥammad al-Shaybānī declares in his *Kitāb al-Āthār* that a *murtaddah* will not be killed but only imprisoned till she either repents or dies.[14] Imām Abū Yūsuf has expressed a similar opinion in his *Kitāb al-Kharāj*.[15] The Mālikī Ibn Qudāmah, in his *Al-Mughnī*, says that a *muḥāribah* woman is not to be killed but only imprisoned.[16]

There are other recognised exceptions that still further restrict the scope of this tradition. Dr Muhammad Hamidullah, in his *Muslim Conduct of State*, has summarised the position in these words:

> In case an insane person, a delirious, a melancholy, a perplexed man, a minor, one intoxicated or who had declared his faith in Islam under coercion and a person whose faith in Islam has not been known or established, were to become apostate, they would not suffer the supreme penalty. So, too, an apostate woman and a hermaphrodite, according to the Ḥanafī school of Law, would not be condemned to death but imprisoned and even physically tortured. An old man from whom no offspring is expected is also excepted.[17]

In support of this statement he refers to al-Kāsānī, *Al-Badā'i*, VII, 134; al-Sarakhsī, *Al-Mabsūṭ*, X, 123; Ibn 'Ābidīn, *Radd al-*

---

13. Al-'Aynī, *'Umdat al-Qārī*, XI–XIII, 232 and 239; 'Asqalānī, *Fatḥ al-Bārī*, XII, 220–28: and *Hidāyah ma'a al-Kifāyah*, II, 200 *et seq.*
14. Urdu trans. by Abu al-Fath Muhammad Saghir al-Din, pp. 222-223.
15. *Islām kā Niẓām-i Maḥāṣil* (Urdu trans. by Muhammad Nijatullah Siddiqi), p. 502.
16. 3rd ed., VIII, 123.
17. 5th ed., pp. 172 *et seq.*

Muḥtār, III 246 and 326–371; Abū Yūsuf al-Kharāj, p. 111; al-Sarakhsī, *Sharḥ al-Uṣūl*, Chapter "*Al-Juz' Yalḥaqahu al-Takdhīb*". These exemptions also find mention in various chapters of *Aḥkām al-Murtadd* by al-Sāmarā'ī. The *Fatḥ al-Bārī* too adverts to two exceptions, *viz.*, of a hypocrite and one forced to the faith.[18] Al-Sāmarā'ī also says that if an apostate comes as an ambassador or messenger on behalf of infidels, then he would not be killed for the Prophet spared the lives of Musaylimah's messengers.[19]

If then the accepted position be that the *ḥadīth* is not to be taken literally and is subject to several qualifications and the circumstances in which the relevant words were uttered by the Prophet are not precisely known, would it be too much to take the next step and suggest that there is also underlying the *ḥadīth* a tacit assumption that the person concerned must be guilty of *muḥāribah* (active hostility)? This would have the merit of bringing the purport of the *ḥadīth* into conformity with verse 34 of Sūrah al-Mā'dah:

> The only reward of those who wage war against Allah and His Messenger and strive to create disorder in the land is that they may be slain or crucified...

That this suggestion is not a novel one would be borne out by what several Doctors of Law have already indicated as the basis for the death penalty in their writings. In the *Hidāyah*, Marghinānī, while discussing the question whether it is necessary to allow time for repentance to an apostate or not, says:

> And for us there is the word of God, "Kill the polytheists ..." without restriction as to time for repentance and so also is the saying of the Prophet (on him be peace): "Whosoever changes his faith, slay him," and that is because he is a *kāfir ḥarbī* [a disbeliever and active rebel] whom the call has reached. He would,

---

18. XII, 220–228.
19. *op. cit.*, p. 211.

therefore, be killed instantly without time being allowed for repentance...[20]

This opinion is further elaborated and confirmed in the *Mabsūṭ*,[21] the *Baḥr al-Rā'iq*,[22] the *Fatḥ al-Qadīr* and by the commentaries of al-Chalpī and al-Bābartī.[23] It is explained in these books that the exemption in favour of a woman is grounded on the fact that she is incapable of bearing arms, normally. Further, it is said that disbelief intrinsically does not justify condemnation to death and that is the genesis of the rule that the blind and the very old will not be killed. A woman apostate may, however, be slain, if she possesses independent judgement and has a following. Al-Zayla'ī in his commentary on the *Kanz al-Daqā'iq*[24] says explicitly: "The reference in the *ḥadīth* is to one who fights against us ..." Marghinānī too observes in the *Hidāyah*[25] that the punishments are postponed to the Hereafter, as their acceleration (and implementation in this world) would interfere with the significance of trial and testing (in this life). The killing of the apostate is said to be necessary to remove the evil of his *ḥirāb* and not on account of his change of faith. For the punishment for apostasy is higher than that in the eye of Allah. The inconsistency between this position and the attempt to equate apostasy itself with *ḥirāb* by these scholars seems to be unaccountable ambivalence. This identity is denied by most authorities as has been specified in Chapter I. It is also noteworthy that Imām Mālik and his associates interpret the word *muḥārib* as one who bears arms against the community in

---

20. II, Bāb "*Aḥkām al-Murtaddīn*," 200 *et seq.*
21. Al-Sarakhsī, al-Mabsūṭ, X, 98–124.
22. Ibn Nujaym al-Miṣrī, *Al-Baḥr al-Rā'iq*, V, 139.
23. *Fatḥ al-Qadīr 'alā al-Hidāyah* with *'Ināyah* of al-Bābartī, and marginal comments of al-Chalpī, IV, 388–389.
24. *Sharḥ al-Zayla'ī 'alā Kanz al-Daqā'iq*, 111, 285.
25. See note 20.

connection with the exegetic gloss on Qur'anic verse 5:33. This is borne out by what is said in the *Baḥr al-Muḥīṭ* (III, 470–471). This view will be reinforced when we consider the various versions of the next tradition to be discussed.

Among other reasons given by him for doubting the authenticity of the *ḥadīth* under discussion, Nawab A'zam Yar Jang[26] (Mawlawi Charagh 'Ali) mentions that there is a gap between 'Ikramah and Ibn 'Abbās and again between the latter and the Prophet, in the chain of narrators. The criticism has weight specially as this *ḥadīth* is of the *aḥād* category. Moreover, 'Ikramah is regarded as an unreliable reporter.

But an alternative approach has been to interpret the word *'uqtulūhu* (kill him) occurring in the *ḥadīth*, not literally, but figuratively, and precedents are cited in support of this suggestion. When the Banī Isrā'īl had taken to the worship of the calf, according to the well-known narrative in the Qur'an (Sūrah al-Baqarah), Moses advised them "to turn to their Maker" and added *"faqtulū anfusakūm"* which may mean, if taken literally, "kill yourselves," but has been interpreted by some commentators as an admonition to kill their evil passions. Reference may be made in this connection, *inter alia*, to *Al-Baḥr al-Muḥīṭ*.[27] Again, on the Prophet's death on the day of *al-Thaqīfah*, when there was a gathering of the Anṣār, at which the chief of the Khazraj named Sa'd set himself up as a candidate for the Caliphate, 'Umar is said to have called out *"uqtulū Sa'd, qatalahu Allāh"*. In this sentence the word *"uqtulū"* which literally means "kill" has been construed as meaning "treat him as if he is dead and do not advert to what he says," in the *Aqrab*

---

26. *Proposed Political, Legal and Social Reforms under Muslim Rule—A'zam al-Kalām fī Irtiqā' al-Islām*: Urdu translation by M. 'Abd al-Ḥaqq, pp. 86 *et seq.*

27. Ibn Ḥayyān, *Al-Baḥr al-Muḥīṭ*, I, 208–209.

al-Mawārid and of *Al-Nihāyah* of Ibn Kathīr. The same authorities assign a similar meaning to the word *"uqtulū"* occurring in the *hadīth*: "If two Caliphs have obtained allegiance (from the people), treat one of them as if he is dead (*uqtulū*), and ignore his claim." One of the meanings assigned to the expression *"qatli al-nafs"* in the *Mufradāt* by Imām Rāghib Iṣfahānī is "killing the base passions".

However, this line of reasoning may not be apt, if a variant of this *hadīth* as given by Imām Mālik in his *Al-Muwaṭṭa'* (Chapter headed *"Al-Qaḍā' fī man Irtada 'an al-Islām"*) is read with it. [28] The wording therein given is *"man ghayyara dīnahu faḍribū 'unuqahū"*—"Whosoever changes his faith, smite his neck". These words are not equivocal and would not leave room for any metaphorical construction. But Imām Mālik adds the comment after giving the *hadīth* that if a Muslim adopts another creed but conceals his disbelief and professes Islam outwardly, then, on proof of his guilt, he shall be slain, without opportunity for repentance being conceded to him, on the ground that such people cannot be trusted. The opportunity to repent, according to him, would be valid only in the case of one who openly adopts another faith, having accepted Islam. This opinion, with all respect for the high status, piety and learning of Imām Mālik, one may venture to suggest, would apparently be inconsistent with the treatment meted out to known hypocrites during the Prophet's time and to the *hadīth* according to which the Prophet had chided Usāmah bin Zayd on his admission that he had killed a man of the Juhaynah tribe in combat, even after he had recited the *Kalimah* (Declaration of Faith). Usāmah pleaded that the man has done so merely to save his life and the Prophet queried: "Did you dissect his heart and look into it?" The

---

28. Imām Mālik bin Anas al-Aṣbaḥī, *Al-Muwaṭṭa'*, Part II. p. 165.

tradition in included in *Ṣaḥīḥ al-Bukhārī*[29] as well as in *Ṣaḥīḥ Muslim* and *Mishkāt al-Maṣābīḥ*[30] of Shaykh Walī al-Dīn Muḥammad bin 'Abdullah Khaṭīb 'Umrī with slight variations.

The fact that this *ḥadīth* exists in a verbally different version, though carrying the same sense, may perhaps justify the criticism that narrators may have retained what they understood to be the purport of the tradition and may have failed to recollect the exact words and the full circumstances surrounding the origin of the saying. This consideration may be allowed to fortify the attempt at its reconciliation with the Qur'anic text by evocation of its underlying assumption that the person involved must have joined those warring against the Muslims. This indeed is the approach of Mawlana Thana'ullah to this *ḥadīth* and the *ḥadīth* to be considered next, in *Islām aur Masīḥiyyāt*.[31] He observes that Islam as a polity had to fight for its existence and these two traditions pertain to a situation where a Muslim forsakes Islam and the Muslim community and he would then be presumed to have connections with the enemies of Muslims. In other words, he says, he himself assumes the position of an enemy and the rule laid down in these reports amounts to a law of war.

Section III

The next tradition to be considered has several verbal variants and, in some of them, the additional words are very significant. The formulation by 'Abdullah bin Mas'ūd runs in these terms:

(1) The Prophet (on him be blessings and peace of God) said: It is not lawful to shed the blood of a person professing Islam,

---

29 . *Ṣaḥīḥ al-Bukhārī*, Urdu translation (with Arabic text) by S. Na'ib Husain Naqwi and Muhammad 'Ali, III, 579.
30 . *Mishkāt al-Maṣābīḥ*, Urdu translation (with Arabic text) by S. Na'ib Husain Naqwi and Muhammad 'Ali, II, 10.
31. pp. 202–204.

who testifies that there is no god but Allah and that I am the Messenger of Allah, except in three cases: life for a life, or a married person guilty of adultery or a person who separates from his faith and deserts his community—(al-Bukhārī "*Kitāb al-Diyāt*," "*Bāb al-Nafs bī al-Nafs*").[32] A similar version exists in al-Tirmidhī's *Sunan* and the collection of Abū Dāwūd.

(2) In the same "*Kitāb al-Diyāt*," "*Bāb al-Qasāmah*," records another version narrated by Abū Qulābah: "The Messenger did not put to death anyone by way of *ḥadd* (prescribed punishment) except for one of three antecedents: a person who commits murder of his own free will shall be killed, (so also) a person who commits fornication after marriage or a person who fights Allah and His Messenger and becomes an apostate from Islam.[33]

(3) A summary version is attributed to 'Ā'ishah in *Sunan al-Nasā'ī*, in which the relevant words for the third category of persons are 'one who commits apostasy, after accepting Islam". A fuller version is, however, also contained in al-Nasā'ī's *Sunan*, which brings out the element of hostility to the community on the part of the apostate.[34] An alternative detailed version is assigned to 'Ā'ishah by Abū Dāwūd ("*Kitāb al-Ḥudūd*," "*Bāb al-Ḥukm fī man Irtaddah*").[35] Therein the third category is defined as comprising a person "*muḥāriban lillāhi wa Rasūlihi fa 'innahu yuqtalu 'aw yuṣlabu 'aw yunfa min al-Arḍi*," ie., "who fights Allah and His Messenger and he will be killed or crucified or banished from the land"—words reminiscent of verse 33 of Sūrah al-Mā'idah.

---

32. *Ṣaḥīḥ al-Bukhārī*, II, 1016.
33. *Ibid.*, II, 1019.
34. *Sunan al-Nasā'ī*, II, 161, 236.
35. *Sunan Abū Dāwūd*, IV, 180.

(4) Two versions are traced to 'Uthmān, the Third Caliph. One says: "I heard the Messenger of God (on him be peace and blessings of God) say: It is not lawful to shed the blood of a Muslim except in one out of three cases: a person who apostatises after accepting Islam or who fornicates after marriage or one who kills a person without retaliation for murder of another" (al-Nasā'ī, *Sunan*: "*Bāb dhikr mā yuḥillu bihi dam al-Muslim*"). In the second version attributed to 'Uthmān, also in the same *Bāb* in al-Nasā'ī, the relevant words are: "Or one who commits apostasy after having believed". It is said that 'Uthmān had proclaimed this tradition to the crowd that had surrounded his house in order to assassinate him.

(5) Somewhat akin to the theme of this *ḥadīth* is the one given by Abū Dāwūd on the authority of Jarīr: 'When a servant of God runs away to polytheism, shedding of his blood becomes lawful." In the *Zamīndār* of 8 October 1924, M. Siraj Ahmad mentions a version included in the *Sunan* of al-Nasā'ī in which the relevant words are: "One who leaves the community and cuts it asunder". There are some lesser compilations of *Ḥadīth* which mention similar versions, but they need not be noticed.

Al-Sāmarā'ī has discussed the tradition traced to 'Uthmān in his *Aḥkām al-Murtadd*.[36] He quotes the opinion of al-Shawkānī from his *Nayl al-Awṭār* (VII, 7), with reference to Ibn Mas'ūd's version of the *ḥadīth* that the words '*al-mufāriq li al-Jamā'ah*" occurring therein mean "one who separates from the Islamic community," and that, according to him, is only possible with *kufr* (disbelief) and not merely by committing an offence or resorting to an innovation, etc. He adds further that this forsaking of the community "must be for joining the disbelievers' community". He also gives an extract from al-Ṣan'ānī's *Al-*

---

36. pp. 40–42.

'Iddah 'alā Iḥkām al-Aḥkām endorsing this view. Al-Ṣan'ānī further observes that there is difference of opinion between the Doctors of Law as to whether a woman should be killed for apostasy or not. The view receives some enforcement from the comment of Ibn Mājah in his *Sunan*, "*Bāb al-Murtadd*," to the effect that no action is to be accepted from a person who has become a polytheist after accepting Islam, until he leaves the *mushrikīn* (polytheists) to rejoin the Muslim community.[37]

In view of the variations in different versions of the *ḥadīth* it may be legitimate to infer that some of the narrators merely recollected its general sense without preserving the verbal integrity of the *ḥadīth*. As Imām al-Shāfi'ī has remarked in his *Al-Risālah*,[38] concerning differences in reports from the Prophet:

> Sometimes he (the Prophet) was questioned about something and he used to give a reply in accordance with the question; sometimes the narrator conveyed fully what he had heard and sometimes summarised, so that, on occasions, the full purport was conveyed and, on occasions, this did not happen. Sometimes, a person merely reported that part of *ḥadīth* which the Prophet had uttered as his reply, because he was himself not present when the question was asked and which occasioned the answer.

With such possibilities open, an attempt to read together all these variant versions so as to get the full picture would be a process which would carry us nearer to the truth. It follows that the delinquents contemplated in the *ḥadīth* are those who were not merely renegades from the faith but also in active opposition to the Muslims, having joined the warring disbelievers' camp. Their case would thus fall within the purview of verse 33 of Sūrah al-Mā'idah and their condemnation would be in harmony with the letter as well as the spirit of the Qur'anic text. The

---

37. Ibn Mājah, *Sunan*, "*Bab al-Murtadd*", p. 182.
38. Urdu translation by M. Amjad 'Ali, p. 150.

present writer finds that this view receives corroboration from the opinion of Mawlana Abu al-Wafa' Thana'ullah, as has been mentioned at the end of Section II.

Section IV

Al-Bukhārī in his *Ṣaḥīḥ* has included a tradition from the mouth of Abū Mūsā al-Ash'arī.[39] It is related therein that the Prophet sent Abū Mūsā al-Ash'arī to Yemen as his Governor and, soon after, Mu'ādh bin Jabal was also deputed to go there. Abū Mūsā welcomed him and invited him to sit down. At that time, a Jew had been brought there, under arrest, who had at first become a Muslim but had later reverted to Judaism. Mu'ādh is reported to have declined to sit down unless the apostate Jew was first killed, "in accordance with the judgement of God and His Messenger". His behest was complied with: the Jew was put to death.

Here again we are in the realm of conjecture as to the actual circumstances surrounding apostasy. It is just probable that the Jew had joined the rebel group of Aswad al-'Ansī in Yemen and that he was not punished for defection from the faith alone. Aswad al-'Ansī had set up claim to prophethood and had become an apostate in the Prophet's lifetime. The Christians of Najrān had joined him and they had ousted the Prophet's two appointees to the area, 'Umar bin Ḥazm and Khālid bin Sa'īd bin al-'Āṣ. Aswad had himself occupied Ṣan'ā'.[40] This suggestion gains some strength from the consideration that Mu'ādh had cited the authority of Allah and His Messenger both, in support of his demand for the extreme penalty to be inflicted on the Jew. In the

---

39 *Ṣaḥīḥ al-Bukhārī*, Bāb "*Ḥukum al-Murtadd wa al-Murtaddah wa Istitābatahum*," II, 1023.
40. Dr M. Hamidullah, *Siyāsī Wathīqah jāt* (Urdu translation by M. Yahya Imam Khan Nowshihrwi. pp. 188–189) (with reference to al-Ṭabarī's *History*): Dā'irat al-Ma'ārif al-Islāmiyah, (Urdu), II. 768.

Qur'an, as we have seen, there is no mention of any such punishment for an apostate, but death is to be the portion of a *muḥārib Allāh* (one who fights God, *ie.,* the Muslim community). In the absence of the exact words of the Qur'an or of the Prophet that Muʿādh had in mind, the position remains equivocal and in any event this would be a very weak precedent. If it was a decision based on the personal *ijtihād* (opinion arrived at after considering analogous provisions of the Qur'an or the *Sunnah*) of Muʿādh bin Jabal, it would not be of binding value. Shah Waliyullah in his *Ḥujjat Allāh al-Bālighah*,[41] cites the opinion of ʿAbdullah bin ʿAbbās, ʿAṭāʾ, Mujāhid and Imām Mālik to the effect that, however eminent a personality may be, if certain statements of his are accepted, there may be some other statements attributed to him, which it would be necessary to reject. For there is no man except the Prophet whose every saying would be capable of citation as a conclusive argument. Earlier[42] he expresses the categorical view that the basis of some statements ascribed to *al-Ṣaḥābah* (Companions of the Prophet) is merely "forgetfulness or error". In the *Mukhtaṣar* of Sayyid al-Sharīf al-Jurjānī it is said: "Whatever is related from a *Ṣaḥābī* (Companion), either in the form of a saying or in the shape of action, whether narrated by a continuous chain of narrators or not, is not a binding instance.[43] In the *Qamar al-Aqmār Sharḥ Nūr al-Anwār*[44] it is laid down on the authority of Mawlana ʿAbd al-ʿAli Bahr al-ʿUlum, that the mere possibility that a *Ṣaḥābī* (Companion) might have based himself on what he might have heard from the Prophet does not make it obligatory to follow his opinion. There is also the well-known observation of Imām al-

---

41. Urdu translation by M. ʿAbd al-Rahim I, 677.
42. *Ibid.*, p. 655.
43. As quoted by M. Sher Ali, in his *Qatl-i Murtadd aur Islām*, pp 142–143.
44. *Ibid.*

Shāfi'ī regarding the *Ṣaḥābah*: "They were men and so are we."[45] It is interesting to recall that Mawlana Charagh 'Ali (Nawab A'zam Yar Jang) criticises the decision of Mu'ādh as one in conflict with the Qur'anic text.[46] Another scholar, Professor Qamr al-Din Khan, has in an article published in *The Pakistan Times* (Lahore) of 18 November 1973, cast grave doubt on its authenticity and has adduced several reasons for that view.

What happened exactly on the occasion to which the report relates is also open to some doubt. Al-'Aynī in his *'Umdat al-Qārī* gives varying versions as to whether the Jew was simply put to death or also burnt.[47]

Section V

There are two traditions concerning a woman who is said to have been killed for apostasy, by order of the Prophet. One is traced to 'Ā'ishah which places the incident on the day of Uḥud and the other to Jābir bin 'Abdullah, by al-Dāraquṭnī and al-Bayhaqī. In the chain of narrators pertaining to the tradition from 'Ā'ishah, there occurs the name of Muḥammad bin 'Abd al-Mālik, as the ultimate transmitter. In respect of him, al-Zayla'ī, the author of *Naṣb al-Rāyah lī Aḥādīth al-Hidāyah*, comments that Aḥmad and others had described him as a fabricator of traditions.[48] The same learned writer criticises Jābir bin 'Abdullah's tradition in the words:[49] And 'Abdullah bin Udhaynah's testimony (he was one of the chain of narrators) has been invalidated by Ibn Ḥabbān. He says: It is not permissible to base an argument on him in this

---

45. *Ibid.*, and *Ḥujjat Allāh al-Bālighah*, Urdu trans., Pt. I Ch. III, p. 668.
46. Nawab A'zam Yar Jang (M. Charagh 'Ali), *Proposed Political, Legal and Social Reforms under Muslim Rule*, Urdu translation: *A'zam al-Kalām fī Irtiqā' al-Islām*, by M. 'Abd al-Haqq, pp. 86 *et seq.*
47. XI–XII, 235.
48. See Part III, Bāb "*Aḥkām al-Murtaddīn*".
49. *Ibid.*

situation, and in *Al-Mu'talif wa al-Mukhtalif,* al-Dāraquṭnī has characterised him as 'one rejected". Ibn 'Adī has related this *ḥadīth* in his *Al-Kāmil* and commented: 'Abdullah bin 'Aṭārid bin Udhaynah is not acknowledged in respect of Ḥadīth and I have not seen our predecessors say anything against this." Mawlana Muhammad Hasan Sunbuli in his marginal comments on the *Hidāyah* of al-Marghinānī has also criticised this *ḥadīth* as "of weak authority" on similar grounds.[50] Both these traditions, therefore, are of doubtful authenticity. In any event, they are vague and indefinite formulations, furnishing no details of the woman involved. It is pertinent to advert to the fact that al-Zayla'ī[51] has also cited two other *aḥādīth*, in one of which the words ascribed to the Prophet are: "Do not kill the woman, if she commits apostasy." This too has been included in Dāraquṭnī's compilation of Traditions. However, the compiler describes the principal narrator, 'Abdullah bin 'Īsā al-Jazrī, as a liar. The other *ḥadīth* is from *Al-Kāmil* of Ibn 'Adī, traced from Abū Hurayrah, and says that a woman who became an apostate was not killed by the Prophet. This is also attacked as of weak authority. Apparently on this point, conflicting but weak traditions are not scarce.

There is one other tradition having a bearing on this subject, in which the woman has been named as Umm Marwān. She was said to have been put to death under orders of the Prophet. It is included in Dāraquṭnī's "Collection", being traced to Jābir. The last transmitter in the chain of narrators is Ma'mar bin Bakkār who is said to be of imaginative type by al-'Uqaylī, according to the author of *Naṣb al-Rāyah.*[52] But even if this tradition is accepted as authentic, there is evidence available which

---

50. *Al-Hidāyah.* II, 355.
51. *Naṣb al-Rāyah,* Pt. III, Bāb *"Aḥkām al-Murtaddīn".*
52. *Ibid.*

differentiates the case from that of a mere apostate. She was actively hostile to the Muslims. Al-Sarakhsī, in his *Al-Mabṣūṭ*,[53] informs us that she partook in actual fighting against Muslims and exhorted others to join the warring group and that she had a following. It was, therefore, for her conduct as a *muḥāribah* (an active oppositionist) that she was put to death, rather than for her change of faith. Some authorities from the school of thought which exempts female apostates from being killed have already been noticed earlier and they would serve to strengthen the inference open on the above discussion that there is no clear warrant for holding that the Prophet had ordered the killing of a woman for apostasy simpliciter. Instances of the Prophet forbidding slaughter of women even in battle would be found summarised in al-Sāmarā'ī's *Aḥkām al-Murtadd*, where the prohibition is stated to be grounded on lack of capacity of females for fighting.[54]

Section VI

The instance of 'Abdullah bin Abī Sarḥ is also mentioned by one Pakistani scholar[55] as lending support to his thesis that the punishment of apostasy is death. The instance, when considered in all its bearings, seems to negative that proposition. Two versions are extracted from the *Sunan* of Abū Dāwūd, "*Kitāb al-Ḥudūd*," Bāb "*Al-Ḥukum fī man Irtadda*". In the first version, it is said that this man took shelter with 'Uthmān, on whose intercession the Prophet pardoned him. According to the second version, 'Uthmān requested the Prophet three times, repeatedly, to accept his allegiance and the Prophet apparently reluctantly

---

53. X, 108–110.
54. pp. 219–220.
55. M. Abul A'la Mawdudi, *Murtadd kī Sazā Islāmī Qānūn min.* pp. 16–18.

acceded to the request, for he later turned to his Companions and said: "Was there no rightly-guided person among you who could have risen to kill this man, seeing that I was withholding my hand from his allegiance?" The Companions are reported to have said that they could not know what was in the mind of the Prophet unless he had himself given them an indication by a wink of his eye. The Prophet told them that it was not becoming a Prophet to have made such a stealthy sign with his eye.

The facts of this case are given by al-Ṭabarī[56] and Ibn al-Athīr[57] in their *Histories* and they are also mentioned by al-Rāzī[58] in his *Al-Tafsīr al-Kabīr* and by Muḥammad Ḥusayn Haykal in his *Life of the Prophet*.[59] After accepting Islam, he used to act as one the scribes for taking down the Qur'anic verses revealed to the Prophet from time to time. He became a renegade and joined the polytheist Quraysh before whom he boasted that he used to write what was dictated to him by the Prophet as and where he liked. He was one of those under sentence of death by order of the Prophet at the time of the Conquest of Makkah. 'Abdullah was a foster-brother of 'Uthmān and that is why he gave him shelter and interceded successfully on his behalf with the Prophet. He was under the sentence apparently for his political crime in making common cause with the enemies of the Muslims and not for mere apostasy. For if he was liable to *al-ḥadd al-Shar'ī* for that offence, it is unlikely that 'Uthmān should have given him protection. It is a well-recognised principle of Islamic *fiqh* that a *ḥadd* once incurred does not lapse. Reference

---

56. Urdu translation by S. Muhammad Ibrahim Nadwi, I, 400 *et seq.*
57. Urdu translation by M. Maqsud 'Ali Khayrabadi, II, 407 *et seq.*
58. V, 527.
59. *Ḥayāt-i Muḥammad* (Urdu translation: *Sīrat al-Rasūl* by Muhammad Warith Kamil), p. 256.

in this context may be made to *Al-Tashrīḥ al-Janā'ī al-Islāmī* of
'Abd al-Qādir 'Ūdah,[60] and *Rūḥ al-Ma'ānī* of al-Ālūsī.[61] The fact
that he received such protection strongly suggests that his
proclaimed punishment was not with reference to his apostasy
but to his association with and encouragement of polytheist
belligerents.

There were actually ten or twelve persons in all who were
under the sentence of death, if captured for their oppositionist
role at that time. They were, besides Ibn Abī Sarḥ, 'Abdullah bin
Khaṭāl, 'Ikrimah bin Abī Jahl, Ḥuwayrith bin Naqīdh, Maqīs bin
Ṣubābah, Ḥibār bin al-Aswad, Ka'b bin Zuhayr, Hind bint
'Utbah (wife of Abū Sufyān, who had mutilated the dead body of
the Prophet's uncle Ḥamzah, in the Battle of Uḥud), Waḥshī bin
Ḥarb, Ṣafwān bin Umayyah and 'Abdullah bin Zab'ar Sahmī.
They were all persons who had either persecuted the Muslims or
fought against them. Waḥshī had killed Ḥamzah by hurling his
weapon at him from a distance. Ibn Khaṭāl had become a Muslim
but had run away after killing a *Ṣaḥābī* or, according to one
version, a Muslim slave. He used to revile the Prophet in verses
that were sung by his two slave-girls—these girls, according to
Ibn al-Athīr, were among those under sentence of death, *in
absentia*. Ka'b and Ḥuwayrith were also charged with similar
abusive and vilifying roles. Ḥibār had attacked the camel
carrying Zaynab, daughter of the Prophet, in collaboration with
Ḥuwayrith, and the latter also attacked the camel on which two
other daughters of the Prophet, Fāṭimah and Umm Kulthūm,
were travelling and, in both cases, the riders had fallen off their
mounts and received injuries. Maqīs bin Ṣubābah had become a
renegade, but he was not immediately interfered with. He was
killed during the Conquest by Ghīlah bin 'Abdullah al-Kalbī.

---

60. *Al-Juz' al-Awwal, al-Ṭab'ah al-Thāniyyah*, p. 79.
61. VI, 188-122.

Maqīs had earlier killed an Anṣārī Muslim who had killed a brother of Maqīs, under a misapprehension—*khaṭā'an*—and he then had run away and defected from the Muslim community. Zurqānī in his *Sharḥ al-Mawāhib al-Laduniyyah* has also given their histories. [62] Some details about these persons are also furnished by Ibn Hishām in his *Al-Sīrah*. [63] However, only four of these persons were eventually killed, the rest, receiving pardon from the Prophet, including Waḥshī, the killer of Ḥamzah. Their offences lay in the political rather than the religious field. It cannot be maintained, in consequence, that the case of Ibn Abī Sarḥ is, in any sense, an apt illustration of the liability of an apostate to the supreme penalty.

The attempt by some writers to draw strength for their contention that death is the prescribed punishment for apostasy, from the incident relating to 'Ukl or 'Uraynah people, must also founder on the rock of differentiating facts. The relevant *ḥadīth* is set out in *Ṣaḥīḥ al-Bukhārī*[64] and *Ṣaḥīḥ Muslim*.[65] It is traced from Anas. The circumstances in which these persons from 'Ukl were killed have already been referred to, while commenting on verse 33 of Sūrah al-Mā'idah, and they are detailed in several commentaries of the Qur'an, *eg.,* al-Ālūsī's *Rūḥ al-Ma'ānī*, al-Suyūṭī's *Lubāb al-Nuqūl fī Asbāb al-Nuzūl*, al-Rāzī's *Al-Tafsīr al-Kabīr*, and others. They were guilty of brutal murder combined with robbery, and they were dealt with on that basis and not for apostasy alone.

Another reported *ḥadīth* ascribes instructions issued by the Prophet to Mu'ādh bin Jabal when he was leaving for Yemen

---

62. Zurqānī, *Al-Mawāhib al-Laduniyyah*, II, 321 (as quoted by M. Sher Ali) and *Al-Kāmil* (Maqsud 'Ali's trans.), pp. 408–409.

63. II, 69–78.

64. Urdu translation (with Arabic text) by S. Na'ib Naqwi and Muhammad 'Ali, III, 587.

65. Part I, Vol. II, Bāb "*Ḥukum al-Murtadd wa al-Murtaddīn*," p. 93.

that both male and female apostates were to be killed unless they repented. In his marginal comment on this *ḥadīth*, M. Muhammad Hasan al-Sunbali,[66] in his edition of the *Hidāyah*, has criticised this *ḥadīth* as resting on weak authority as its narrators are questionable.

It is claimed that a woman who was abusing the Prophet was killed by a *Ṣaḥābī* and the Prophet remitted her *qiṣāṣ* (punishment for murder). The tradition is included in the *Sunan* of Abū Dāwūd and is said to have been narrated by 'Ikrimah and al-Sha'bī. Doubt has been cast on its authenticity by criticism of al-Nasā'ī, among others, of 'Uthmān al-Shaḥām, one of the narrators, as a weak link. Al-Sha'bī's version is also not accepted as authentic as, according to al-Ḥakim, he had not heard a single tradition from 'Alī whom be had claimed as the source of information for this *ḥadīth*. Apart from this aspect of the matter, however, the death of the woman was caused under circumstances of grave provocation offered by her to Muslims, and if the Prophet, as Head of the State, remitted the punishment, the instance cannot be put forward to buttress the contention that apostasy had to be punished with death. In this connection, it would be pertinent to refer to another *ḥadīth* included in *Ṣaḥīḥ al-Bukhārī*. It is reported that a Jew, while passing by the Prophet, had said: "*al-sa'mu 'alaykum*" (death on you). The Prophet merely retorted back: "*wa 'alayk*" (and on you). When the people around asked for permission of the Prophet to kill him, he forbade them from doing so.[67] So apparently such kind of provocative conduct was also to be ignored.

Abū Dāwūd's collection contains a *ḥadīth* which is to the effect that if a slave runs away to polytheism (*shirk*), strike his

---

66. *Al-Hidāyah* (with marginal gloss by Muhammad Hasan al-Sunbali, III, 354, marginal note.
67. Urdu translation (with Arabic text) by S. Na'ib Naqwi and Muḥammad 'Ali, III, 598.

neck, it is obvious that the phrase "runs away to polytheism" means that he goes and joins the *mushrikīn* who were always at loggerheads with the Muslims. This does not, therefore, pertain to a case of apostasy simpliciter. This was one of the instances cited by M. Muhammad Shafiʻ, in support of the death penalty for an apostate, in his article published in the *Zamīndār* of 23 and 24 October 1924.

Section VII

As we have seen, none of the *aḥādīth*, normally relied on by the protagonists of the penalty, unequivocally support that judgement. That they should not be so construed is a suggestion that has much to commend itself in view of what follows.

A *ḥadīth* is related from Jābir bin ʻAbdullah in *Ṣaḥīḥ al-Bukhārī*,[68] by three different chain of narrators, to the effect that a Bedouin Arab accepted Islam and took the oath of fealty on the Prophet's hand. Soon after, he contracted high fever and came back to the Prophet to demand cancellation of his allegiance. He repeated this demand three times but each time it was refused. He then went away—apparently unmolested. The Prophet merely remarked that Madīnah is like a furnace which separates the dross from what is pure. If apostasy had to be visited with the death sentence, he should not have been allowed to depart with immunity. There is also a discussion of this *ḥadīth* in the *Fatḥ al-Bārī*.[69]

Interesting light is thrown on the question we are considering by clauses (4) and (5) of the Ḥudaybiyah Peace Pact, concluded between the Muslims acting through the Prophet and the

---

68. *Ibid.*, III, 689–91.
69. Ibn Ḥajar al-ʻAsqālānī, *Fatḥ al-Bārī*, XIII, 173.

polytheist Quraysh of Makkah through their plenipotentiary, Suhaīl bin 'Umar. These clauses are reproduced below[70]:

4. If a Makkan becomes a Muslim, without the permission of his family chief and migrates to Madīna, it will be obligatory for Muḥammad to return him to Makkah.

5. In the reverse case, if someone from Madīnah defects from Islam and seeks protection in Makkah, the Quraish would not return him.

If the apostate Muslim was liable to the death sentence, it is extremely unlikely that such a provision should have been agreed to, in derogation of a commandment of the *Sharī'ah*.

In the Madīnah Pact which in effect was a federal type of constitution for the government of Madīnah headed by the Holy Prophet, clauses 20 and 21 read as follows:

20. In case peace is concluded with an enemy, the benefits if any accruing thereby will be shared by the other parties to the Pact in the same way as the Muslims would do.

21. But for a person who becomes an apostate from his religion, this door will be barred.

Here it is noteworthy that the only disadvantage to be suffered by an apostate was deprivation of benefits derived under a Peace Pact with an enemy and there is not even a hint that an apostate was liable to be decapitated.[71]

Again, in the document of *amān* (protection) granted to the Ḥadas branch of the Lakhm tribe by the Prophet[72] and scribed by 'Abdullah bin Zayd, it is provided that in respect of members of the tribe who accept Islam, keep up prayer, pay the *zakāh* and the Prophet's share and give up friendly relations with the polytheists, the responsibility to protect their lives, their property

---

70 Dr M. Hamidullah, *op. cit.*, Urdu translation by M. Abu Yahya Imam Khan Nuwshihrawi, p. 53.

71. *Ibid.*, pp. 19–24.

72. *Ibid.*, pp. 65–66.

and their honour will rest on Allah and His Messenger (*ie.*, on the Muslims):

> But if any one of them, after becoming a Muslim, commits apostasy, then the responsibility of Allah and His Messenger will cease with regard to him, and a person who authenticates his Islam by his actions will have his faith certified by the Prophet.

Nothing was said to indicate that apostasy would invite the capital sentence—only he would lose his protective cover.

It is also possible to gain some guidance on the point in question from the dialogue that took place between Abū Sufyān (who was then a non-Muslim) and the Caesar of Byzantium, whom the Arabs give the name "Hiraql" (Heracles). Abū Sufyān was accompanied by his Quraysh companions and one of the questions put by the King to Abū Sufyān was whether any of the followers of the Prophet was known to have become a renegade from his faith. The answer was in the negative. Here was an occasion for Abū Sufyān to have assigned this steadfastness to the threat of the extreme penalty for apostasy if such had been the case—he was no friendly emissary who could suppress such a fact. The absence of such a charge is significant.[73]

When *Qiblah* for prayers was changed, by Divine Command, from Bayt al-Maqdis to the Ka'bah at Makkah, the decision came as a shock to the Jews and even to some Muslims. The incident is referred to in the opening verse of Part II of the Qur'an and it is explained in verse 144 of Sūrah al-Baqarah that the change was effected so that Allah "might know him who follows the Messenger from him who turns upon his heel". Ibn Jarīr al-Ṭabarī in his commentary *Jāmi' al-Bayān* mentions that some of the Muslims had actually defected from Islam on this the

---

73. Ibn al-Athīr, *Al-Kāmil*, Urdu translation by Maqsud 'Ali Khayrabadi, p. 344.

occasion.[74] He quotes the comment of Ibn Jurayj that these apostates said: "Once it is here and another time it is here"—objecting to the change of *Qiblah*. There is no indication given, however, that these apostates were punished for their defection, nor do the relevant Qur'anic verses point to any such dispensation.

There is apparently some difference of opinions between scholars as to whether *al-Isrā'* (which is mentioned in Sūrah Banī Isrā'īl) and *al-Mi'rāj* (to which reference exists in Sūrah al-Najm) are two separate phenomena or they both represent one single experience of the Prophet. *Al-Isrā'* means the night-journey which the Prophet is said to have performed from Makkah to Jerusalem and back in one night and *al-Mi'rāj* is the ascension to the Heavens and the experiences related to it. Both Ibn Hishām[75] and Ibn al-Athīr[76] have given the Prophet's account of his experiences in this regard and some of the people who heard of this claim made by the Prophet turned apostates. Ibn Hishām has cited the opinion of Ḥasan in this context that the Qur'anic verse:

> And We appointed the vision which We showed thee as an ordeal
> for mankind, and (likewise) the Accursed Tree in the Qur'an.
> (17: 60)

was revealed in respect of those who became apostates on this occasion. None of the historians, however, has mentioned any attempt being made to bring the offenders to book by any pressure or punishment. Al-Sāmarā'ī has also referred to this incident in his *Aḥkām al-Murtadd*[77] in an extract from the *Musnad* of Aḥmad who mentions that these apostates were killed along with Abū Jahl (in the Battle of Badr) but evidently not sentenced to death after adjudication.

---

74. II, 8.
75. *Sīrat*, Urdu translation by Qutb al-Din Ahmad Mahmudi, II, 7 *et seq.*
76. *Al-Kāmil*, Urdu translation by Maqsud 'Ali Khayrabadi, II, 64–72.
77. p. 35.

The treatment of hypocrites by the Prophet, in spite of their identity being known, has already received attention earlier during the discussion on the position of apostates under the Qur'an. A single instance in this connection is that of Julās bin Suwayd bin al-Ṣāmit. As related by Ibn Hishām, he had lagged behind when the Prophet had proceeded with his Companions for the Expedition to Tabūk. Not only that, but he gave out that "if this person [meaning the Prophet] had been right, we should have been worse than asses". This was conveyed to the Prophet, but Julās, when questioned, swore falsely that he had said nothing.[78] On this the *āyah* was revealed:

> They swear by Allah that they said nothing (wrong), yet they did say the word of disbelief, and did disbelieve after their surrender (to Allah). And they purposed that which they could not attain, and they sought revenge only that Allah by His Messenger should enrich them of His bounty. If they repent, it will be better for them, and if they turn away, Allah will afflict them with a painful doom in this world and the Hereafter, and they have no protecting friend or helper in the earth (9:74).

He, too, in spite of his proclaimed disbelief in the word of God, was apparently not killed for his apostasy. Indeed Ibn Isḥāq is reported to have said that he, later on, repented and became a good Muslim.

Shah Waliyullah in his *Ḥujjat Allāh al-Bālighah*[79] has referred to the strange case of a person who became a *murtadd* in the Prophet's time. He died, and, when buried, the earth "did not accept him but threw out his dead body". Probably he had in mind a *ḥadīth* included in al-Bukhārī's *Ṣaḥīḥ* and traced to Anas.[80] It is related therein that a Christian became a Muslim,

---

78. *Sīrat*, Urdu translation, *op. cit.*, pp. 203–205.
79. Urdu translation, *op. cit.*, II, 822.
80. Ra'īs Aḥmad Ja'farī, *op. cit.*, p. 359.

learnt Sūrah al-Baqarah and Āl 'Imrān from the Prophet and became one of the scribes of the revelations. He later reverted to his original faith and bragged that the Prophet knew only as much as he had written out for him. Sometime after, he died (evidently a natural death) and was buried. His dead body was seen to have been cast out of his gave the day after his burial. This time he was buried even deeper into the ground but the same strange phenomenon occurred again. The deceased's relatives suspected that the Prophet's followers had a hand in this mysterious incident. He was again buried and this time at a much greater depth under ground. Lo! and behold! his body was found thrown out again and people were now convinced that this was not due to human action. The point of this *ḥadīth* is that the man was not put to death for his apostasy which was even accompanied by grave provocation to the Muslims.

In the sixth year of the Hijrah, according to Ibn al-Athīr, Mujjā'ah bin Murārah who had come as a member of a delegation from Hawdhah bin 'Alī, King of Yamāmah, became a Muslim. He, however, went back, defected from the faith and even brought up a false accusation against the Prophet that the latter had taken Musaylimah al-Kadhdhāb as his partner. There is, however, no mention of any attempt being made to punish him.[81]

Professor Heffening, in his article on "Murtadd" in the *Encyclopaedia of Islam* (1932 edition), says "there are traditions according to which even the Prophet forgave apostates," and he cites al-Nasā'ī ("*Taḥrīm al-Dam*", *Bāb* 14, 15), Abū Dāwūd ("*Al-Ḥudūd*", *Bāb* 1), Ibn Ḥanbal (I, 247) and *Tafsīr al-Ṭabarī* (III, 223), in support of this view. This remark and the other positive instances of absence of action against apostates, adduced above, negative the contention of those who urge that the Prophet

---

81. Ibn al-Athīr, *al-Kāmil*, Urdu translation, *op. cit.*, II, 350.

had determined the punishment for apostasy to be death, as a part of the religious dispensation, *stricto sensu.*

It has been seen that even the strongest bulwark of the orthodox view, *viz.,* the *Sunnah,* when subjected to critical examination in the light of history, does not fortify the stand of those who seek to establish that a Muslim who commits apostasy must be condemned to his death for his change of belief alone. In instances in which apparently such a punishment was inflicted, other factors have been found to co-exist, which would have justified action in the interest of collective security. As against them, some positive instances of tolerance of defections from the Faith, with impunity for the renegades, suggest that the Prophet acted strictly in conformity with the letter and the spirit of the Qur'an, and mere change of faith, if peaceful, cannot be visited with any punishment. The sayings of the Prophet, on which the whole edifice of orthodox reasoning is raised, in the absence of a knowledge of the surrounding circumstances, must be construed in sense which would make them consistent with the Book of Allah, for it is unimaginable that the Prophet could have gone against any Qur'anic text. There is no doubt a section of *'Ulamā'* who make the *Sunnah* the final arbiter in every case seeming or real conflict with the Qur'an—their claim is: "*Al-Sunnah Qāḍiyah 'alā al-Kitāb*"—the *Sunnah* is the judge over the Book. This is not accepted by some of the best minds among the Muslim scholars, past and present, and such a doctrine would indeed strike an unconscionable blow at the integrity and pristine purity of the Qur'an. For instance, Imām al-Shāṭibī in his *Al-Muwāfaqāt* explains that this dictum merely means that the *Sunnah* explains the Qur'an and it is not intended to lay down that it takes precedence over the Book of God.[82]

---

82. *Al-Muwāfaqāt, al-Juz' al-Rābi', Mas'alah Thāniyyah,* as quoted in M. Taqi Amini, *Aḥkām-i Shar'iyyah min Ḥālāt wa Zamānah kī Ri'āyat,* p. 314.

CHAPTER III

Apostasy and the *Khilāfah al-Rāshidah*

Section I

It is asserted that a woman named Umm Furqah ordered to be killed by Abū Bakr (the First Caliph) for apostasy. But this is based on a misconception. She was not merely an apostate but a rebel who exhorted her thirty sons to war with the Muslims.[1] She would be, therefore, legitimately classified as a *muḥāribbah* herself.

Much is made by those who favour the death sentence for apostasy of the wars of Abū Bakr with the *murtaddīn*. Al-Rāzī in his *Al-Tafsīr al-Kabīr*[2] has given a list of eleven tribes that had defected from Islam, three of them having done so in the Prophet's own time and eight in that of Abū Bakr's. The first tribe to commit apostasy was Banū Madlaj whose chief was Aswad al-ʿAnsī, in Yemen. As has been mentioned already, he had rebelled against the State and ejected the Prophet's *ʿāmilīn* (officials) from several cities. The Prophet had written to his Governor in Yemen, Muʿādh bin Jabal, and other chiefs of Yemen to counter his movement and Aswad was killed. Banū Ḥanīfah was the tribe of Musaylimah al-Kadhdhāb who had the effrontery to write to the Prophet to ask for half the land of

---

1. Al-Sāmarā'ī, *Aḥkām al-Murtadd*, p. 220; al-Sarakhsī, *Al-Mabṣūṭ*, X, 110.
2. III. 415.

Arabia for himself. When rebuffed, he rose in revolt, set himself up as a prophet and made common cause with another pretender, a woman named Sajāḥ bint al-Ḥārith. He had ousted Thumāmah bin Āthāl, the appointee of the Prophet, from governorship and assumed rulership of Ḥijāz and Yamāmah. He killed Ḥabīb bin Zayd, a *Ṣaḥābī*, who had refused to accept his claim as prophet, mutilated his body and then burnt it. Action had already started against him in the Prophet's lifetime, but his movement was liquidated in the time of Abū Bakr at the Battle of Yamāmah. The third tribe that became apostate in the Prophet's lifetime was Banū Asad, Ṭulayḥah bin Khuwaylid al-Asadī being their chief. He too raised an army and tortured the Muslims he captured to death. He was defeated by Khālid bin al-Walīd, during Abū Bakr's regime. He ran away to Syria and later turned a Muslim. Laqīṭ bin Mālik al-Azdī also became an apostate and arrogated to himself the status of a prophet. He too rebelled and usurped the rulership of Oman. Military action was eminently justified against all these persons.

Al-Ṭabarī has given a full account of all these rebel tribes who had refused to pay *zakāh* and defied the State officials. Apparently 'Umar had his doubts about the legitimacy of the war against those tribes whose members still recited the declaration of faith though they had declined to pay *zakāh*. Abū Bakr reassured him by declaring that he would fight those who differentiated between prayer and *zakāh*, for the latter was *ḥaqq al-māl* (due on property, to be exacted by the State).[3] 'Umar agreed with Abū Bakr. *Zakāh* was collected as a State impost during the Prophet's time as well as during the *Khilāfah al-Rāshidah*. The Qur'an directs the Prophet to "take alms out of

---

3. *Ṣaḥīḥ al-Bukhārī*: Urdu translation (wit Arabic text) by S. Na'ib Naqwi and M. Muhammad 'Ali, III, 597.

their wealth (of those who repented of their sins) so that thou mayest cleanse them and purify them thereby" (9:103). There is also a *ḥadīth* in Bukkārī in which describes *zakāh* as wealth "which is taken from the rich and returned to the poor". Mawlana Muhammad 'Ali in *The Religion of Islam* says about *zakāh*: "It is a State institution, or where there is no Muslim State, a national institution."[4] Dr. M. Hamidullah in his article on Jurisprudence in *A History of Muslims Philosophy*, has also expressed the opinion that *zakāh* is not almsgiving or charity but a State tax or duty.[5] Al-Mawārdī in his *Al-Aḥkām al-Sulṭāniyyah* says that a person who refuses to make over *zakāh* to the just *Imām*, though accepting its validity, is a rebel against the community and war against him could be legitimately waged.[6]

Actually this was not a simple case of defiance of one particular commandment of God—the conduct of the tribes amounted to rebellion and they resorted to actual armed attacks on Muslims, as al-Ṭabarī clarifies.[7] The initiative in the fighting was taken by the tribes of 'Abas and Dubyān and Abū Bakr had to fight them before Usāmah had returned from the campaign to which he had been assigned. The other tribes followed suit and gathered in force at Dhī al-Qiṣṣah. Khārijah bin Ḥassīn had advanced on the Muslims to take them by surprise. After Abū Bakr had refused the demand for exemption from *zakāh*, made by some tribes, they had actually invaded Madīnah. Abū Bakr had himself warned the Muslims of the impending attack in these words: "The land (*ie.,* people) has become apostate and their delegations have seen that you are small in number. You do not

---

4. p. 467.
5. M.M. Sharif, Ed., II, 1224 and 1231.
6. p. 47, as quoted in Muhammad Taqi Amini, *Aḥkām-i Shar'iyyah min Ḥālāt wa Zamānh kī Ri'āyat*, p 52.
7. *Ta'rīkh* (E.J. Brill ed.), IV, 1872–1877 *et seq.*, 1900 and 1960.

know whether you might be attacked by night or by day…" They actually attacked Madīnah three days later, leaving a group of fighters in Dhī al-Ḥussī. They had killed the staunch Muslims who were still living among them, earlier. In the *'Umdat al-Qārī* it is also stated by al-'Aynī:

> And al-Ṣiddīq [Abū Bakr] fought those who refused to pay *zakāh* because they had taken up the sword and started a war against the *ummah*.[8]

Al-Ṭabarī further elucidates [9] that Khālid bin al-Walīd refused to pardon the recalcitrant *murtaddīn* unless they had first surrendered those of their number who had burnt to death Muslims or mutilated their bodies. The tribe of Banū Rabī'ah had set up a new king in the person of Mundhir bin al-Nu'mān, known as Maghrūr, in Hīrah.

Professors Wellhausen and Caetani have expressed the opinion that these were purely political rebellions having not much connection with religion. Their article on *"Ṣiddīqi Akbar"* in the latest edition of the *Encyclopaedia of Islam* may be referred to in this context. In the face of the facts detailed above, the plea of those who maintain that these people were merely guilty of non-compliance with a tenet of Islam cannot be sustained.

Mawlana Sa'id Ahmad Akbarabadi, in his book *Ṣiddīqi Akbar*, has approached this subject from another angle.[10] He thinks that tribes who refused to pay the *zakāh* did so under the influence of their tribalism (*'aṣabiyyah*) as they apprehended that after the Prophet's demise they would be relegated to the inferior position of the tributaries of the Islamic State. In reality, according to the learned author, they were not *murtaddīn*

---

8. XI–XII, p. 236.
9. *op. cit.*, IV, 1872–1877, 1900, 1960.
10. pp. 149, 161.

(apostates) in the strict sense and that is why 'Umar and some other Companions gave expression to their doubt about the propriety of making war on them. There were others, however, he says, like the followers of Ṭalḥah (or Ṭulayḥah) and Musaylimah who had never been genuine Muslims but had accepted, for a time, the hegemony of the Islamic State. He expresses his conclusion in these words: "In the first place, this was not a case of *irtidād* (apostasy) and, if it was, then it was more of a political than a religious defection. That is to say, these people, as a matter of expediency, had agreed to give political allegiance to the Prophet, remaining hypocrites at heart. Subsequently they busied themselves in intrigues and when the conditions were favourable, they openly raised the banner of revolt."

Al-Ṭabarānī[11] mentions in his "History" that Abū Bakr had pardoned 'Ayniyyah bin Ḥiṣn and Qurrah bin Habīrah who had been captured by the Muslims, although 'Ayniyyah had declared that he had till then not believed in God, and Qurrah had also secretly become an apostate, though he adopted hypocrisy in this regard. The treatment of these two persons indicates the absence of any settled rule for the punishment of apostates or hypocrites.

This historical perspective thus yields no indication that the first Caliph had acted on the principle that a change of faith, even though peaceful, would require to be suppressed by force. His wars were waged against active rebels.

Section II

Kanz al-'Ummāl[12] includes a report (relied upon by some scholars) to the following effect: 'Amr bin al-'Āṣ, the governor of Egypt, wrote to 'Umar, the Second Caliph, that a person had

---

11. *Ta'rīkh*, Urdu translation by S. Ibrahim Nadwi, Part III, p. 78.
12. Shaykh 'Alī Muttaqī, *Kanz al-'Ummāl*: Urdu translation by S. Farid al-Din alias Achchu Mian, p. 508.

accepted Islam but had reverted to disbelief. He again came back to the Islamic fold but became a renegade a second time. He had been oscillating between the two faiths a number of times and now finally wanted to rejoin the Muslim community. The Governor asked for advice as to what should be done in such a case. 'Umar is said to have replied that his Islam "should be accepted as long as Allah accepts it"—so long as he goes on repenting, his profession should be accepted as valid. It was added by the Caliph in his reply that if, after presentation of Islam, he declines to follow it, they should smite his neck. The first part of the advice makes it clear that repeated apostasies were to be tolerated. The second part, in the absence of a clear authority from the Qur'an or the *Sunnah*, may be demurred to, with the highest respect for the great Caliph, in the same spirit in which a woman had dared to contradict him, by citing a verse of the Qur'an, when he wanted to limit women's dower by an order. The *Kanz al-'Ummāl*, moreover, is a collection of *Ḥadīth* on which not much reliance is placed by adepts in the subject. However, the report could be reconciled with the Qur'anic text and the Prophet's *Sunnah*, if it is presumed that each time the man defected, he joined the enemy ranks.

The second incident of 'Umar's time, to which reference is generally made is that, after the conquest of Tustar, Sa'd bin Abī Waqqāṣ and Abū Mūsā al-Ash'arī had sent a messenger to the Caliph. Among other things, the messenger reported that they had caught an Arab who had committed apostasy after becoming a Muslim and had killed him. 'Umar said: "Why did you not do this? You should have shut him up in a room, bolted the door and given him one loaf of bread on each of three days. He might possibly have repented in that time. O God! This was not done under my orders, nor was it done in my presence, nor was I pleased when I heard it." It is emphasised, however, that Sa'd and Abū Mūsā were not called to account for what they had done and the Caliph's comments merely established the desirability of opportunity being allowed for repentance. This dialogue between 'Umar and the messenger is given by Abū Ja'far al-Ṭaḥāwī in *Sharḥ Ma'ānī al-Āthār*[13] and also by Ibn al-Athīr al-Jazrī in his *Jāmi' al-Fawā'id*.[14] It is, moreover, said to be mentioned in al-Shāfi'ī's *Kitāb al-Umm* and *Al-Muwaṭṭa"* of al-Bayhaqī. As for the three days' grace period, the question will be discussed hereinafter.

Al-Ṭaḥāwī's compilation referred to above recounts another incident connected with what happened during the conquest of Tustar. Anas came as the emissary of Abū Mūsā to the Caliph 'Umar who inquired as to what had befallen Ḥajībah and his companions and also about the people of Bakr bin Wā'il. They had become apostates and joined the polytheists. They were killed by the Muslims, apparently in a fight, and when this was reported to the Caliph, he observed that they should have caught them alive for that would have been more pleasing to him than any valuables. The emissary said: "O Commander of the Faithful! what could have been done to them except that they should have been killed, if they were captured alive?" The Caliph replied: "If you had taken them alive, I would have presented to them the door by which they had gone out (of Islam). If they had reverted (to Islam), well and good, otherwise I would have consigned them to prison." Apparently these people had been killed in regular battle as al-Bayhaqī clarifies in *Al-Sunan al-Kubrā*, "*Kitāb al-Murtadd*".[15] In spite of that, the Caliph, it seems, would have merely imprisoned them unless they

---

13. II, 117–121; al-Bayhaqī, *Al-Sunan al-Kubrā*, VIII, 207.
14. pp. 282–283.
15. VIII, 207.

repented—there is no indication here that he would have killed them. This report, therefore, seems to detract from the value of the precedent dealt with above. For these people were not simple apostates—they had, in addition, fought the Muslims, and if such leniency could be shown in their case, *a fortiori*, greater leniency would have been possible in respect of mere apostasy unaccompanied by *ḥirāb* (active enmity). In the alternative, an assumption ought to be made that even in the instance cited above the persons concerned were *muḥāribs* (active oppositionists) and not mere renegades from the faith.

The third incident of the Second Caliph's time, on which reliance is placed by some writers on the subject of apostasy, relates to the case of 'Abdullah bin al-Nawāḥah. It was reported to 'Abdullah bin Mas'ūd that some people sitting in a mosque of Banī Ḥanīfah were declaring Musaylimah to be a prophet. They were sent for by 'Abdullah bin Mas'ūd and they all expressed penitence. Out of them, 'Abdullah bin al-Nawāḥah was ordered to be killed, but the rest were allowed to go away. 'Abdullah bin Mas'ūd explained that Ibn Nawāḥah was one of two persons who had come as envoys of Musaylimah to the Messenger of God. On the Prophet's query whether they would testify to his prophethood, the two envoys put the counter question: Do you testify that Musaylimah is God's messenger? On this the Messenger of God observed that if it had been permissible to kill delegates, he would have ordered both of them to be slain. They were, however, allowed to depart without molestation, as envoys were entitled to protection. It was because of this remark of the Prophet that 'Abdullah bin Mas'ūd had ordered that he be put to death. One scholar thinks that as 'Abdullah bin Mas'ūd was Chief Qāḍī of Kūfah under 'Umar at that time and his action was apparently condoned by the Caliph, it should be accepted as a precedent favouring death for an apostate.[16] It may, however, be pointed out that if Ibn Nawāḥah was also penitent along with his companions, the Chief Qāḍī was under a religious obligation to accept his *tawbah*, even according to the orthodox view. In so far as he departed from this norm, his personal decision cannot he upheld as a binding precedent. Moreover, the Prophet himself had stayed his hand out of respect for his status as envoy and one fails to see how words uttered by him in that capacity would make him liable to the supreme penalty, if he was subsequently captured, in another context. The Prophet's observation on that occasion should have been accepted on its face value as conferring immunity on the man despite his obnoxious conduct. In any event, this incident cannot be used as a precedent for ordering the death sentence for apostasy. Musaylimah, it may be remembered, was a pseudo-prophet and a rebel against the Muslims, and this would also reflect on his adherents.

There is also the instance quoted from 'Abd al-Razzāq's compilation of Ḥadīth, of an *umm walad* (a female slave who had borne a child to her master) turning Christian. 'Umar ordered her to be sold to people other than her own co-religionists.[17] If as an apostate she was liable to the death sentence, this decision would be hard to understand. It can only be reconciled with the assumption that there was no such prescribed punishment.

As in the case of the Prophet himself, 'Umar too had written to the Christian residents of Najrān, before their banishment, to the effect that any of them accepting Christianity instead of Islam would lose his protection. They had, it is to be remembered, reverted to Christianity after once joining the Islamic fold.[18] No

---

16. M. Abul A'la Mawdudi, *Murtadd kī Sazā Islāmī Qānūn min*, pp. 20–21.
17. Al-Zayla'ī, *Naṣb al-Rāyah li Aḥādīth al-Hidāyah* p. 100.
18. Dr M. Hamidullah, *Siyāsī Wathīqah Jāt*: Urdu translation by Abu Yahya Imam Khan Nuwshihrawi, pp. 115–116.

threat of execution was held out to actual or prospective apostates. This conduct on the part of the Caliph can be of assistance in evaluating the other instances mentioned and would suggest the inference that the element of *ḥirāb* (active enmity) must be presumed to exist in those instances in which the death penalty was actually imposed.

Section III

This brings us to a consideration of instances from 'Uthmān's regime. These find place in lesser known compilations of Ḥadīth like al-Bayhaqī's "Collection", and the *Kanz al-'Ummāl*. They belong to the category not considered reliable by discerning scholars like Shah Waliyullah of Delhi.

The first relevant entry in *Kanz al-'Ummāl* ascribes a statement to 'Uthmān, on the authority of the *Musnad* of 'Uthmān, that whosoever becomes a disbeliever after having voluntarily adopted the Faith, he would be killed.[19] This is a bare statement without any information as to the circumstances in which the words were uttered by the Caliph and without reference to any authority in the Qur'an or the *Sunnah*. Not much weight can be attached to such abstract sayings, and, if at all, they should be construed as qualified by the requirement of *ḥirāb* on part of the person concerned. That would reconcile the saying with the letter and spirit of the Qur'an.

The second instance in the *Kanz*[20] is a report from Sulaymān bin Mūsā that 'Uthmān had called upon a *murtadd* three times to recant and then ordered him to be killed, as he refused to comply with the demand. Here, again, the brief account almost amounts to an inferential statement from circumstances that are shrouded

---

19. Urdu translation, *op. cit.*, p. 511.
20. *Ibid.*, p. 512.

in darkness. For all one knows, the man in question may have been a rebel besides being a renegade from the Faith.

Then finally we have the version of 'Abdullah bin Mas'ūd in the *Kanz*[21] that a group of people in Iraq committed apostasy. He wrote to Caliph 'Uthmān regarding them and received the reply that Islam should be presented to them, and if they agreed to accept the Faith, they should be left alone. If they refused, they should be fought against (*qātalakum*) as given in one version by a writer in the *Zamīndār*. This is clear indication that these people were rebels against whom military measures were taken and the instance, therefore, does not warrant the conclusion that peaceful apostasy by itself would have been regarded as punishable.

A review of these cases would not justify the enunciation of a positive principle that even in a case of apostasy, not accompanied by active hostility, the Third Caliph would have ordered the person concerned to be slain. The sayings are bereft of the circumstantial details such as could lend colour to such an inference.

Section IV

'Alī's war with the Khawārij (the seceders) is used by some writers as evidence to justify the view that an apostate deserves to be killed. The question whether the Khawārij must be regarded as merely errant Muslims, or a group altogether outside the pale of Islam, seems to have been a matter of controversy between the Doctors of Law. But 'Alī's own opinion appears to have been that they had not ceased to be Muslims. In *Al-Musawwā min Aḥādīth al-Muwaṭṭa'*,[22] Shah Waliyullah has recorded a report

---

21. *Ibid.*, p. 514.
22. II, 290–291.

that the Fourth Caliph heard a man proclaim near a mosque: *"Lā ḥukm illā li Allāh"*—there is no judgement except that of God—which was the slogan raised by the Khawārij against 'Alī for his having agreed to arbitration between him and Mu'āwiyah, in respect of succession to the Caliphate. 'Alī acknowledged that what the man was saying was correct and told him that he had three things to offer them: (*i*) they will not be prevented from the mosques so that they may remember Allah therein; (*ii*) they will not be prevented from sharing in *fay'* (The booty that accrues Muslim warriors, without fighting) so long as their hands were with his hands (another version varies this condition to: Whatever they earn will be immune from *fay'*); and (*iii*) the Caliph will not initiate the fighting with them. The implication is clear that 'Alī did not regard them as disbelievers. The fighting between the Caliph's forces and the Khawārij resulted from their stand that those who did not share their beliefs were liable to be killed as disbelievers and they actually killed some Muslims who had passed by them, on this plea. Details of their attitude and the consequent fighting are given by several historians including Ibn al-Ṭiqṭiqā (*Al-Fakhrī*)[23] and Ibn al-Athīr (*Al-Ta'rīkh*).[24] Reference may also be made for support to this view to the *Fatḥ al-Bārī*.[25] M. Sher 'Ali also quotes from *Al-Tafsīr al-Kabīr*[26] to show that most *'Ulamā'* regarded the Khawārij to be a sect of the Muslims, despite their doctrinal aberrations. Their case is, moreover, distinguishable from that of peaceful apostates because of their taking up arms against the Muslims. No benefit can be gained by sponsors of the punishment theory of apostasy from such an instance.

There is also a report from 'Ikrimah, a freed slave of Ibn 'Abbās, that 'Alī had ordered the burning to death of certain

---

23. pp. 114–117.
24. III, 148 *et seq.*, as in Sher 'Ali's book.
25. XII, 267–268.
26. III, 614, quoted in *Qatl-i Murtadd aur Islām*, p. 164.

heretics (*zanādiqah*). Ibn 'Abbās heard of this incident and remarked that he would have put them to the sword and not subjected them to torture by fire for that method of punishment was forbidden by the Prophet. He then recited the *ḥadīth*: "Whosoever changes his faith shall be killed." This report is included in *Ṣaḥīḥ al-Bukhārī*.[27]

Al-'Aynī in his *'Umdat al-Qārī* cites an opinion that those persons were followers of Ibn Sabā' who invested 'Alī 'with divine status.[28] M. Sher 'Ali has cited[29] excerpts from Ibn Ḥazm's *Al-Faṣl fī al-Milal wa al-Ahwā' wa al-Niḥal* and al-Shahrastānī's *Al-Milal wa al-Niḥal* which confirm the nefarious role of these people in attempting to create dissensions among Muslims. On the authority of al-Shahrastānī, it is stated by M. Sher 'Ali that 'Alī had banished Ibn Sabā' to Madā'in on his saying to the Caliph: "*Anta anta*" (You are, you are—God). So the Sabā'is were disrupters of the social order and their case would be differentiated from that of simple apostasy, on that ground.

Moreover, Mawlana Abu al-Jalal Nadawi A'zamgarhi[30] criticises this report on technical grounds. He says that Ibn 'Umar and Sa'īd bin Muṣayyab charged 'Ikrimah with *kidhb* (lying) and Ibn Mu'īn did not accept traditions from him as he belonged to the Ṣafariyyah sect of the Khawārij. His attribution of an act to 'Alī, which was against an injunction issued by the Prophet, is, therefore, open to doubt. According to 'Abdullah bin al-Ḥārith, Imām Ḥusayn, son of 'Alī charged 'Ikrimah with fabricating reports against his father[31] and people did not offer funeral prayers for him when he died. Apart from the question of

---

27. Arabic-Urdu, *op. cit.*, III, 596.
28. Al-'Aynī, *'Umdat al-Qārī*, XI–XII, 234.
29. Quoted in his *Qatl-i Murtadd aur Islām*, p. 67, from Ibn Ḥazm's *Al-Faṣl*, II, 115, and al-Shahrastānī's *Al-Milal* on the margin of Ibn Ḥazm's *Al-Faṣl*, p. 167.
30. *Qatil-i Murtadd*, p. 13.
31. Jalal al-Din Shams, *Islām aur Madhhabī Āzādī*, pp. 126–128.

its authenticity, however, the aptness of this precedent is also questionable, as shown above.

Kanz al-'Ummāl gives another report[32] from Abī Ṭufayl. He was included in an expedition sent by 'Alī against Banī Najiyyah. They found them divided into three groups. One group among them said they were Christians initially but had accepted Islam and had held fast to it. The second group declared that they had adhered to their original faith, Christianity. The third group, after becoming Muslims, had reverted to the Christian creed. When called upon to return to Islam, they declined the offer and they were killed in the fighting that ensued and their families were made slaves. It is apparent that this was a case of rebellion combined with apostasy. An expeditionary force had to be sent against them and they were killed in the fighting. The instance does not serve to strengthen the stand of those who would like to make out apostasy to be a crime rather than a sinful transgression.

The same collection of Ḥadīth[33] mentions one al-Mastūr or al-Mastūrad bin Qabīṣah as having become a renegade from Islam to Christianity. He admitted this fact when brought before 'Alī but he evidently, in the course of conversation with the Caliph, whispered "'Alī, 'Alī" (God's name) in his ear which led to his being killed. This detracts from the value of this precedent for, it seems, his attribution of Divine status to 'Alī led to the decision given therein. For all we know, he may also have been a *muḥārib*, for not much is mentioned about his history.

Both the above two instances are, otherwise too, of weak authority, for they are part of a compilation which does not inspire consummate confidence in its reliability.

---

32. Urdu translation, *op. cit.*, pp. 517–518.
33. *Ibid.*

An anonymous writer in the daily *Zamīndār* dated 11 October 1924, on the authority of *Sunan al-Nasā'ī* and some lesser known compilations, also referred to the rebellion of the people of Ḥirārā. It is said that 'Alī sent Ibn 'Abbās and some other Companions and Anṣār in a delegation to them and two thousands of the rebels reverted to the true faith on their persuasion and the rest were killed. It is clear that here there was a combination of apostasy with rebellion and the instance is not pertinent to the question whether apostasy alone requires to be punished.

A review of the relevant reports pertaining to the *Khilāfah al-Rāshidah* thus reveals some incidents which included an element of active hostility to Muslims, justifying active violence against persons who had combined apostasy with rebellion. Other incidents in which apparently apostates were punished are either based on reports of dubious authority or, being bereft of antecedent details, do not suffice to furnish adequate guidance as to the rule that should prevail in such cases. In some instances we have merely verbal reports about what was said or done by one of the four rightly-guided Caliphs on some occasion, without any attempt at analysis of the factors that determined the saying or the deed. On the other hand, the absence of action or suggested action in certain instances would seem to militate against the assumption that there was any firmly-established and well-defined precedent governing such cases. There is room for raising a presumption in most cases that the delinquent who came in for punishment might have transgressed the bounds of good citizenship or tried to harm the collective interests of the Muslim community and was thus adjudged guilty of an offence calling for extreme treatment by the persons in authority, by the way of *ta'zīr*.

CHAPTER IV

Apostasy and the *Fuqahā'*

At the outset, it may be acknowledged that the apparent unanimity among *al-Fuqahā'* on the question of treatment to be meted out to an apostate from Islam strikes one, at first sight, as impressive. Differences, however, exist, firstly, as to whether it is incumbent on the adjudicating authority to afford an opportunity for repentance to the apostate before he is condemned to death and, secondly, as to whether female apostates are to be exempted from this punishment or not. By analogy, some other exemptions have also been the subject of juristic discussions. A useful summary of the principal points involved and the variant opinions expressed thereon would be found in al-Sāmarā'ī's *Aḥkām al-Murtadd*.[1] The significance of these differences and their impact on the main point, whether apostasy is a culpable offence, will become apparent after we have surveyed the whole field and are in a position to comment on the rationale of juristic opinion.

The first question formulated by al-Sāmarā'ī, in this context, reads:

> When a Muslim commits apostasy, is he to be killed after proof of his apostasy has become available (forthwith) or is he to be called upon to repent? And if he insists on his apostasy, is he to be put to death or given a respite?

---

1. pp. 194–222.

The learned author notes that there has been a good deal of controversy between those who deny the necessity of a demand being made for reversion to the Faith and those who are convinced of the obligatory nature of such a step. He quotes from the *Raḥmat al-Ummah fī Ikhtilāf al-A'immah* of al-Dimashqī an extract which epitomises the differences on this point. The latter starts by saying that the *A'immah* are agreed on the proposition that whosoever forsakes Islam would be liable to the death sentence. Then the consequent procedural steps which have evoked controversy are commented upon. According to him, Imām Abū Ḥanīfah's position was that *istitābah* (calling for repentance) was not obligatory and the person concerned should be put to death unless he himself asks for consideration, in which case three days' grace period would be allowed to him. Some of the Imām's followers, however, have opined that even if no respite is solicited, a period of grace should be granted by way of *istitābah* (as a course recommended). Imām Mālik considered a demand for *tawbah* (repentance) to be obligatory. If the person repents, his *tawbah* should be accepted. If he is adamant, he should nevertheless receive a respite for three days for he might possibly relent during this period. If he insists on his apostasy after that, he would be killed. To Imām al-Shāfi'ī two differing opinions are ascribed on both points, of the necessity for *istitābah* and the grace period. Imām Aḥmad bin Ḥanbal is also attributed two variant opinions. It is related from al-Ḥasan al-Baṣrī that there should be no *istitābah* and the person should be slain immediately. 'Aṭā' makes a distinction between a person born a Muslim and a disbeliever accepting and then becoming a renegade. In the case of the former, no demand for repentance would be made, but in the case of the latter, this would be necessary. There seems to be apparently no rational basis for such a distinction. From Sufyān al-Thawrī the tradition has been handed down that the opportunity for repentance should extend over the lifetime of the delinquent, and this was also the opinion of Ibrāhīm al-Nakhaʿī who was the teacher of the teacher of Imām Abū Ḥanīfah. Ibn Qudāmah[2] interprets this dictum of al-Nakhaʿī to mean that the apostate can never be killed (*Lā yuqtal abadan*). Imām al-Shaʿrānī has also summarised the various opinions about the necessity or otherwise of allowing time for repentance to an apostate. He also prominently mentions the opinion of al-Thawrī that an apostate will be given the respite for all time and not killed. His words are: *"wa qawl al-Thawrī fīhi takhfīf min ḥaythi innahu yustatābu abadan wa lā yuqtal."*[3] Imām al-Shaʿrānī belonged to the Shāfiʿī school.

From among the Imāmiyyah, al-Ṭūsī has expressed the opinion that the call for repentance should be made twice and that this was necessary. He has, however, stated in another place that there was no legal justification for fixing any time-limit for repentance and has cited an instance wherein ʿAlī had demanded reversion to the Faith from a Muslim who had become a Christian and, as he declined the offer, he was killed. Referring to the *ḥadīth* "Whosoever changes his Faith shall be killed," he has explained that it apparently did not sanction a demand for repentance. Somewhat inconsistently, al-Ṭūsī in a later part of his book, *Tahdhīb al-Aḥkām*, has cited a report from Sahl bin Ziyād that ʿAlī had prescribed a three days' grace period after a demand for repentance had been made. Al-Naḥwī and al-Sayāghī from among the Zaydiyyah favour three days' respite after the call for *tawbah*.

Imām Ibn Taymiyyah did not regard it obligatory to make a call for repentance before inflicting the penalty of death for apostasy. He derived strength for his view from the tradition

---

2. *Al-Mughnī*, VIII 125.
3. *Al-Mizān al-Kubrā*, II, 152.

which says that a person who quits the Faith and separates himself from the Islamic community is liable to be killed, and added that the Prophet had not prescribed *istitābah*, though he directed that if such a person repents, he is to be left unmolested. The reason is that the call to the Faith had already reached him earlier, as contrasted with the case of a *kāfir aṣlī*—a disbeliever continuing as such. Apparently Imām Ibn Taymiyyah also considered that the cases of Ibn Abī Sarḥ, Maqīs bin Ṣubābah, 'Abdullah bin Khaṭāl, and others, and the people of 'Uraynah supported his stand. Al-Sāmarā'ī himself observes that these instances are not apt as they are distinguishable on facts and the persons concerned were guilty of active opposition to Islam or had murdered Muslims, and these were not instances of simple apostasy. We have also discussed these cases earlier and arrived at a similar conclusion. They were more akin to highwaymen. Al-Sāmarā'ī also mentions that the Prophet adjudged four persons for death penalty as they had defected from the Faith and in addition had reviled the Prophet and defamed him as well as the Faith. But he adds the significant comment that he did not kill them all and accepted repentance from some of them. He expresses the definite opinion that an apostate is not like a highwayman.

In this context, the opinion of Ibn Qudāmah al-Ḥanbalī is also quoted from his *Al-Mughnī* to the effect that respite is the right of the apostate for this might reform him.

The opinion of al-Sarakhsī (Ḥanafī) is then cited from his *Al-Mabsūṭ* that the respite of three days is based on the analogy of *khiyār*—option of rejection, in a sale transaction, within three days. The analogy is by no means helpful, for a conversion or reversion to a creed, being a matter of conscience, cannot be equated with a profane sale transaction which connotes a dealing between two persons, for a consideration. Al-Sarakhsī evidently seeks to follow the practice of 'Umar in allowing a three-day grace period for repentance. Al-Sāmarā'ī also adverts to *Al-Muhallā* of the Ẓāhiriyyah Imām, Ibn Ḥazm, wherein it is mentioned that practice has varied from a three-fold demand for repentance coupled with a respite of three days or even one day's or a whole month's grace period as was apparently adopted by 'Alī, in one case. Al-Sāmarā'ī's own predilection is for the matter of the respite period being left to the discretion of the Imām or sovereign authority, who will determine the issue, having regard to all the circumstances of a case. In any event, he thinks, the period fixed should be adequate for ensuring sufficient time for full consideration of his opinion by the delinquent and that perhaps it would be better not to have a time-limit at all. Specially would the procedure be appropriate, according to him, when a whole group of apostates has to be dealt with collectively, and fortifies himself by citing the opinion of al-Sarakhsī to the same effect that the Imām should have full discretion.

On the authority of *'Umdat al-Qārī, Irshād al-Sārī* (these two being commentaries on *Ṣaḥīḥ al-Bukhārī*) and *Sunan* of Abū Dāwūd with its commentary by al-Suyūṭī, he states that the Prophet himself had accepted the *tawbah* of several apostates. But Ibn Qudāmah al-Ḥanbalī would deny an opportunity for repentance to a *zindīq* (heretic) who conceals his disbelief, for his outward show of belief would not improve matters. Such a stance would seem to run counter to the express injunctions contained in some *aḥādīth* and to the practice of the Prophet in dealing with hypocrites.

Al-Ṣabbāgh, from among the Shāfiʿiyyah, would accept the *tawbah* of a *zindīq* also, for, he says, it is immaterial whether such a person's *kufr* comes out in the open or is concealed. In one of his statements. Imām Aḥmad bin Ḥanbal has drawn on Zaydiyyah view for a similar opinion, in his *Al-Baḥr al-Zakhkhār*. Al-Sāmarā'ī's apparently approves of this stand. The learned author then discusses certain other specific cases, *eg.*, a person who abuses God or His Messenger or is a sorcerer, and quotes opinions of certain jurists that the perpetrators of such offences cannot be forgiven. In support, some of them cite verse 48 from Sūrah al-Nisā':

> Verily Allah forgives not that a partner should be ascribed to Him. He forgives (all) save that to whom He will.

This text would not, in the humble opinion of the present writer, justify the delinquent's punishment, necessarily in this world—like other forms of *kufr* (disbelief).

Al-Sāmarā'ī then takes up the question as to whether *tawbah* of a person who repeatedly changes his faith should be accepted without any limitation or not. This is also a subject of controversy among *Fuqahā'* (jurists). Ibn Qudāmah in his *Al-Mughnī* favours acceptance every time that such an occasion arises and he cites an impressive list of authorities in support of this proposition, though he also notes some dissenting views. He relies on verse 137 of Sūrah al-Nisā': "Lo! those who believe, then disbelieve, and then increase in disbelief, Allah will never pardon them, nor will He guide them to the (right) way," and verse 38 of Sūrah al-Ānfāl: "Tell those who disbelieve that if they cease (from persecution of believers) that which is past will be forgiven them."

Al-Subkī has quoted an opinion from al-Shāfi'ī in his *Al-Sayf al-Maslūl* (to which al-Sāmarā'ī had access, in its manuscript form) that every time an apostate reverts to the Faith, opportunity for repentance has to be allowed and that the Prophet had given such opportunity to one, Rayān, four or five times. He then quotes the opinion of Ibn Wahb that *istitābah* is to be available always and every time there is change of faith, on the authority of Imām al-Shāfi'ī, Imām Aḥmad and Ibn al-Qayyim There are opinions available of Imām al-Shāfi'ī and al-Ṣabbāgh from among Shāfi'īs, of Imām Muḥammad from among the Ḥanafiyyah and Ibn al-Qayyim, in accord with this view, as evidenced by *al-Umm* and *al-Shāmil* (manuscript) of the first two and of *Al-Mabsūṭ* of Imām Muḥammad (manuscript). To Isḥāq he ascribes the view that the apostate must be killed on the fourth occasion of his reversion. The Ḥanbalīs, however, generally, deny opportunity for repentance to a person who repeats his apostasy, and reference is made to *Al-Kāfī* of Ibn Qudāmah, *Muntahā al-Arādāt* of Ibn al-Najjār, *Manār al-Sabīl* of Ibn Dūyān and *Hidāyat al-Rāghib* of 'Uthmān. This opinion they base on verse 137 of Sūrah al-Nisā' set out above and verse 90 of Āl 'Imrān: "Surely those who disbelieve after their belief and then increase in disbelief, their repentance shall not be accepted and these are they who have gone astray," and add that the repetition of their offence indicates the corruption of their creed and their scant regard for Islam.

To the superficial observer, verses 89 and 90 of Sūrah Āl 'Imrān may present a problem in so far as the former talks of God accepting repentance from apostates in general terms, and the latter declares that the *tawbah* of those who increase in disbelief (or, as Pickthall has it, "have grown violent in their disbelief") shall not be accepted. Ibn Jarīr al-Ṭabarī in his *Jāmi' al-Bayān*[4] has tried to resolve the apparent conflict by suggesting that the latter *āyah* applies to Jews who had entertained belief in the advent of the Prophet of Islam but, when

---

4. II, 223–224.

he appeared, they declined to accept him and thus became disbelievers, and that their increase in disbelief refers to sins they committed in that state. It is these sins, according to him, that shall not be forgiven, unless they first discard their disbelief in the Prophet. It is not intended to lay down, he says, that God will not accept genuine repentance after disbelief, from His servants, for He has promised to accept it from all disbelievers or sinners.

Shaykh Ismā'īl al-Ḥaqqī in his *Rūḥ al-Bayān*[5] offers the comment that the verse only means that God will not guide them so long as they persist in their liking for disbelief and when they revert to the truth, they will again receive guidance. As has been observed earlier, the author of *Al-Baḥr al-Muḥīṭ* records the opinion of the meaning of "and who increase in disbelief" is that they complete their disbelief and die as disbelievers—that is to say, these people only would have no forgiveness. "Increase in disbelief" obviously requires an extended period of time for its actualisation.

Al-Rāzī in his *Al-Tafsīr al-Kabīr* has given several alternative Interpretations of verse 90 of Āl 'Imrān, and these have been noticed by us earlier, in the section to Qur'anic *āyāt* bearing on apostasy. Others have also made attempts at reconciliation of these verses. Ḥasan, Qatādah, 'Aṭā' and al-Zamakhsharī say that if an apostate repents on his death-bed, this shall not be accepted from him, on the authority of verse 18 of Sūrah al-Nisā'. Qāḍī 'Abd al-Jabbār and Ibn Qifāl and Ibn al-Anbārī suggest that verse 90 of Āl 'Imrān applies to those who apostatise a second time after reverting to the true Faith—their second apostasy would wipe out the effect of even their first *tawbah*. Another suggestion made by certain scholars is that *tawbah* of those who

---

5. I, 344.

increase in disbelief is not acceptable, as they never repented of their original apostasy.

The words of the *āyah* are, however, general and should be so understood as applying to all *murtaddīn* (apostates) from Islam and the words *ba'da īmānihim* (after they have believed) apply to Muslims who become renegades. Wherever reference is made to Jews and Christians in the Qur'an they are specifically described as *Ahl al-Kitāb* (People of the Scripture). It has been suggested that in verse 90, the non-acceptance should be understood as referring to their first *tawbah*, the effect of which has been taken away by their subsequent perfidious conduct.

Verse 17 of Sūrah al-Nisā' is also pertinent in this context: "Forgiveness is only incumbent on Allah towards those who do evil in ignorance and then repent soon after (*min qarīb*). These are they towards whom Allah relents. Allah is All-Knowing, Wise." The words in the *āyah*, *bi jihālat*, have been rendered as "in ignorance". But the word *jahl* and its derivatives are also used in the Qur'an for acts known to be evil but of whose effects the perpetrator is ignorant. An example is furnished by verse 89 of Sūrah Yūsuf: "He said: 'Do you know what you did to Joseph and his brother, in your ignorance?'" The end-words there are *idh antum jāhilūn*. The brothers of Joseph knew that what they were doing was wrong, though they may not have adverted to its evil consequences. *Kufr* (disbelief) is the highest form of "evil"—*Mufradāt al-Qur'ān* of Imām Rāghib al-Aṣfahānī bears this out. Al-Ṭabarī in his *Jāmi' al-Bayān*[6] cites a saying of Ibn 'Abbās: "Whosoever does an evil act, he is ignorant." Again, the words *min qarīb* which were generally translated as "soon after" have a more comprehensive connotation. Al-Ṭabarī has cited several opinions in his *Jāmi' al-Bayān*[7] that *qarīb* in this verse

---

6. IV, 187.
7. III, 174–176.

means, according to consensus, "time of death"—that is, repent-ance is possible except for an actual death-bed repentance. Al-'Aynī in his *'Umdat al-Qārī*[8] interprets the phrase "increase in disbelief" as meaning that they go on intensifying disbelief till they die and their repentance at the time of death would not be accepted. These comments indicate that the door of repentance is not closed even to hardened disbelievers during their lifetime.

This opinion appears to accord well with the view al-Thawrī, al-Nakha'ī and others that time for repentance must extend over the lifetime of the person concerned and cannot be limited. There is also a *hadīth* narrated by Abū Hurayrah in *Ṣaḥīḥ Muslim* that if a person repents before the sun rises from the west (before Doomsday), God accepts his penitence.[9] That is a forceful way of saying that the possibility of repentance is open throughout the temporal span of human life.

The limitation of the grace period does not reveal a general agreement, even among the *Ṣaḥābah* (Companions) and, evidently, their varying opinions were based on their individual *ijtihād* (judgement). Similar is the case with *fuqahā'* (jurists) who had differing approaches to this question. If we find that any one opinion out of them is more in consonance with the letter and spirit of the Qur'an text and the established practice of the Prophet, we can adopt it as the norm for decision. This procedure would be in keeping with what the great *Imāms* had themselves counselled their followers to do. In he *Ḥujjat Allāh al-Bālighah*,[10] Shah Waliyullah gives an extract from 'Allāmah al-Sha'rānī's *Al-Yuwāqīt wa al-Jawāhir*, which is instructive. Says al-Sha'rānī "This is also reported from the Imām [Abū Ḥanīfah]

---

8. XI-XII, 233.
9. *Mishkāt al-Maṣābīh*—Walī al-Dīn Khaṭīb 'Umrī: Arabic-Urdu by S. Na'ib Naqwi and M. Muhammad 'Ali, I, 523.
10. Urdu trans. by 'Abd al-Rahim, I, 701.

that whenever he expressed an opinion, he would say; 'This is the opinion of Nu'mān bin Thābit. I have exerted to the utmost to arrive at that view which strikes me as best of all. But if someone is in the know of something better, then the correct position would be that that should be followed and what I have said should be discarded.'" Imām Mālik also used to declare "There is no one, except the Messenger of God, among whose sayings there will not be some that are acceptable and some that are worth rejection." Al-Ḥakim and al-Bayḍāwī have also quoted Imām al-Shāfi'ī dictum: 'If you come across an authentic *ḥadīth*, that is my creed also." Similarly, Imām Aḥmad bin Ḥanbal used to say: "As compared with the word of God and of His Messenger, no statement by any other person deserves to be regarded."[11] As we have discussed in the section relating to the Qur'anic texts bearing on apostasy, some of them clearly contemplate the natural death of the apostate in due course, one result of which will be that all his good actions will be wiped out—2:161 and 217, and 3:90.

If then the view of Nakha'ī, and al-Thawrī and others be preferred, that no limitation as to time can be imposed on the time allowed for repentance, on the ground that it is in harmony with the Qur'anic text and not in conflict with the *Sunnah*, it would clearly follow that an apostate cannot be subjected to any pressure, physical or otherwise, nor can he be punished for his peaceful apostasy, though goodly exhortation may be utilised to persuade him to change his belief. For he has a whole lifetime available for reconsideration of his position, short of the actual moment of death.

The question arises: what, then, are the grounds on which the seemingly unanimous opinion of jurists, that an apostate should

---

11. *Ibid.*

be put to death, is based? In his *Aḥkām al-Murtadd*,[12] al-Sāmarā'ī states that apostate has to be killed only by order of the person in authority (*Imām*), for his slaying is obligatory in respect of a right of Allah as contrasted with a private person's right. He makes an exception in favour of a person who acts as an envoy on behalf of disbelievers, for the Messenger of God had forbidden the killing of Musaylimah's envoys. Then the learned author mentions the dialogue between al-Miqdād and the Prophet as to the propriety of killing a disbeliever who, in the course of a fight, declares his faith in Islam and points out that the mere profession of such faith would confer immunity on the person concerned, without any probing into the genuineness of his conversion. He comments that if, by a mere declaration of faith, a person can secure his life, then (it follows that) if he disbelieves in Islam, he should forfeit it, for "whoever has the power to bestow has also the power to take away." This, with all respect, appears to be at best specious reasoning. The analogy of an unconditional gift being withdrawn by a donor would not be apt in such a case. Even if it be true that a man can save his life by a simple declaration of faith, it does not follow that the converse proposition, that a renegade loses his life, should also be true. Here there is an obvious fallacy.

A typical illustration of the orthodox attitude towards apostasy is furnished by the discussion included in al-Sāmarā'ī's book on the position of one who is compelled to accept the true faith.[13] By and large, the opinions collected therein favour the view that if such a person reverts to his original faith, after the compulsive pressure is removed, he would not be regarded as an apostate and would not be liable to punishment. Al-Sarakhsī is

------

12. pp. 211–212.
13. Al-Sāmarā'ī, *op. cit.*, pp. 72–74.

quoted as saying that there was only an outward manifestation of Islam, on his part, under the shadow of the sword and, therefore, inference is that he never really believed. It is strange that an exactly similar situation arising on the *istitābah* of a Muslim who commits apostasy does not attract the same principle in the writings of these savants. Al-Sāmarā'ī's, while agreeing with the dictum of al-Sarakhsī, generally, adds by way of exception that in respect of a *fāriq al-ḥarbī al-murtadd* (a hostile apostate who separates from the community), the acceptance of apparent reversion to the Faith under coercion would be regarded as permissible, for he is compelled to the truth. But that clearly negatives the Qur'anic injunction *Lā ikrāha fī al-Dīn* (there is no compulsion in religion). He enunciates clearly the principle at one place that "one who does not believe in Islam with his heart remains a disbeliever, and he has no share in Islam, irrespective of whether compulsion or coercion is permissible in his case or not, for one cannot attain to Islam, without belief, in a state of full possession of reason". He says further: "Faith is born of belief on the part of an independent person who has unfettered power of choice," and quotes the above verse in support. However, somewhat inconsistently, he adds in the end: "But coercion exercised over an apostate to make him revert to the Faith, on pain of being killed, is an exception, for this is a matter established by *naṣṣ* (well-defined text), and it is not possible to vary that decision by *ijtihād*. The reason he gives for this opinion is that he had voluntarily accepted Islam initially, had become familiar with the Faith and then defected from it, and that is a different case from that of a person who never believed and never accepted Islam under duress. One may wonder why the principle should change in the circumstances visualised, when one remembers that faith has relation to genuine belief and not a mere show of it under coercion.

In the tenth volume of his *Al-Mabsūṭ* in *Bāb "Aḥkām al-Murtaddīn"*, al-Sarakhsī has taken his stand on the Qur'anic verse: "Say unto those of the wandering Arabs who were left behind: You will be called against a folk of mighty prowess, to fight them until they surrender" (48:16), and which was revealed in respect of the apostates, according to one opinion. He also cites the *ḥadīth* "Whosoever changes his faith, slay him," and argues that apostates are worse than polytheists and to the latter the Muslims can offer only one of two alternatives—Islam or the sword. On the last two points enough has been said earlier. According to the generally accepted view, the verse cited concerns those hypocritical bedouin tribes who had contrived to lag behind when the Prophet went to Makkah for the *'Umrah* (lesser pilgrimage) from where he returned with the conclusion of the Peace of Ḥudaybiyah. Exegetists do not, by and large, agree with al-Sarakhsī that the verse refers to *murtaddīn*. The verse, according to the most favoured construction, contains a prophecy that the Muslims would come into conflict with the Byzantine and Iranian Empires whose subjects were people "of mighty powers".[14] Al-Sarakhsī apparently interprets the word *yuslimūna* occurring in the verse as meaning "until they become Muslims" instead of "until they surrender". It is well known that the Iranians and the Byzantines were defeated by the Muslims during 'Umar's time, but they did not immediately become Muslims though they had surrendered to them and become subservient to them.

The suggestion, therefore, that God's word called upon Muslims to fight these peoples till they accepted Islam would be contrary to historical facts and, therefore, the interpretation adopted by most translators that they would become subservient

---

14. Al-Rāzī, *Al-Tafsīr al-Kabīr*, VII, 544.

to the Muslims is to be preferred. The peace treaty of Bayt al-Maqdis was signed between 'Umar and the Byzantines, in the sixteenth year of Hijrah and Iran was conquered in the twenty-first year of Hijrah. Conversions to Islam took place later, during the reign of Marwān bin al-Ḥakam and the regime of 'Umar bin 'Abd al-'Azīz of the Umayyad family. Ibn al-Athīr in his *Al-Nihāyah fī Gharīb al-Ḥadīth* has given one meaning of the word *aslama* to be "he became obedient, or submissive" as in the Prophet's saying in which he declared that there is a Satan with every person, but "I have made my 'Satan' submissive to myself".

Shah Waliyullah in his *Ḥujjat Allāh al-Bālighah* [15] has attempted to justify the orthodox line by observing that apostasy would amount to rank impertinence in respect of God Almighty and would defeat the Divine objective of making truth prevail and of establishing its unquestioned authority. Citing the *ḥadīth* "Whosoever changes his faith must be killed," he explains that, in such a case, it is necessary to subject the renegade from the Faith to condign punishment, for tolerance of such an incident and overlooking it would open the door wide to lowering the prestige of the true Faith and would amount to insulting it. He expresses the view that God Almighty would be pleased if the Faith He has revealed should become (so to speak) man's second nature. The question at once arises whether a coercive process could ensure such a laudable result. And in the face of the explicit Qur'anic verses which have been discussed earlier, is it to be presumed that the defection from the Faith, by an insignificant human, would detract from the majesty of the Self-Sufficient Almighty? If the Qur'anic texts are given their full force, any attempt to coerce a reluctant person to believe would be contrary to the Divine scheme of things.

---

15. Urdu translation, *op. cit.*, II, 661–662.

A modern scholar has offered the following observations in this matter: "Islam is not a religion but a whole way of life.... A community organised as a State can with difficulty find room within its boundaries for people who differ from it on fundamentals which are the basis of that community." Regarding *dhimmīs*, in his opinion, the Islamic State tolerates them and those actions of theirs which do not directly conflict with the basis of the community, "as Islam is not without hope in respect of human nature,"[16] and expects till the last that they may see the light of truth in the end. Again, one might, with respect, query whether human nature ceases to be human nature, in the case of an apostate. The argument is pushed to its logical conclusion by the learned scholar when he postulates that a person who disagrees with the basis of organised society has only two alternatives open to him: he may either go out of the boundaries of the society's operation or submit to deprivation of all rights as a citizen. The latter state, according to him, would be worse than death and, therefore, it would be better to kill him, for a rightless person would be a danger to society.[17] He considers that apostasy in an Islamic State would be tantamount to high treason and that offence, he points out, is punishable with death in all civilised systems of jurisprudence in the West, He cites the cases of Great Britain and America in this context.

The main reason for punishing an apostate is expressed by Al-Sāmarā'ī in these words:

> Again, Islam is not merely a religion but also a nationality, and rebellion against it would mean deprivation of this nationality. For such an act would be treachery and change from co-citizenship to enmity, as has been explained by Shaykh Aḥmad Ibrāhīm (in *Majallat al-Qānūn al-Miṣriyyah*). The apostate causes others to

---

16. Abul A'la Mawdudi, *Murtadd kī Sazā Islāmī Qānūn min*, pp. 45–48.
17. *Ibid.*

imagine that Islam is lacking in goodness and thus prevents them from (accepting) it. Consequently he commits an offence not only against his own person but against others also. A disbeliever, if he sticks to his disbelief, is excusable in the eye of people, for one reason or another. But, after he has been introduced to Islam and has been united with his Maker, what is his excuse? Says Sayyid Quṭub (in his *Fī Ẓilāl al-Qur'ān*): Disbelief that precedes belief is forgiven. For one who has not seen the light may be excused if he walks in darkness. But for disbelief after acceptance of the Faith, there can be no forgiveness and no excuse. Verily disbelief is a veil. When it is lifted man's nature is united with his Maker, the strayed camel is joined to the caravan and the plant is connected with its source-spring. Those who become renegades after that calumniate their nature, deliberately insist on their error and adopt arrogance and waywardness.

There is no forgiveness after that and no guidance. They lead their souls voluntarily towards destruction and specially when apostasy is repeatedly committed by them, after they have believed: "Lo! those who believe, then disbelieve, and then (again) believe, then disbelieve and then increase in disbelief, Allah will never pardon them, nor will He guide them unto a way"—4:137. Their increase in disbelief is the natural result of their backsliding and their straying into error after having received guidance. That is their last opportunity to follow the just and well-defined path.[18]

This kind of reasoning fails to convince the modern mind which is conditioned by rationalism. And Islam being *Dīn al-Fiṭrah*, the religion of Nature, would favour rational thinking. It does not stand to reason that a person who at any time accepts the true faith and is later assailed by doubts should be in a worse position than a confirmed and hardened disbeliever.

The treatment of the question of Nationality in an Islamic State reveals an ambivalent attitude on the part of our jurists. For

---

18. Al-Sāmarā'ī, *op. cit.*, pp. 212-213.

instance, a modern Egyptian jurist, 'Abd al-Qādir 'Ūdah, commits himself to the opinion that all residents of Dār al-Islam have one nationality whether they be Muslims or *dhimmīs*. But then, in all probability, under stress of the generally expressed view that apostasy calls for the death sentence, he seeks to differentiate between Muslim and non-Muslim citizens as regards the basis on which their nationality rests. For Muslim citizens, he considers that the foundation of Nationality is Islam but for non-Muslims allegiance to the State is regarded as a sufficient basis. Consequently, he says, a Muslim loses his nationality on apostasy while a non-Muslim does so by repudiation of the allegiance to the Islamic State and adoption of residence in *Dār al-Ḥarb*.[19]

Under international law, the grant of nationality is within the domestic jurisdiction of the State. But there is no compelling religious reason for departing from the international norm of residence in and allegiance to the State as the criterion of nationality for all subjects. Indeed, that would be, in my humble opinion, in harmony with the tolerant and liberal spirit of the Qur'an and not against the sayings of the Prophet, rightly understood in their historical context. Article 15 of the United Nations General Assembly's Declaration of Human Rights, approved on 10 December 1948, says that everyone has the right to a nationality and that none shall be arbitrarily deprived of his nationality. If a citizen is to be deprived of his nationality on change of faith, even though he may desire to retain his allegiance to the State as a peaceful citizen, it would result in the anomaly of making such a person Stateless. The only grounds mentioned in Articles 8 of the International Convention on the Reduction of Statelessness, of 1961, are that the person has

---

19. 'Abd al-Qādir 'Ūdah, *Al-Tashrī' al-Janā'ī fī al-Islām* (2nd ed.), I, 307–308.

rendered services to or received emoluments from another State or has conducted himself in a manner prejudicial to the vital interests of the State or that the person has taken an oath or made a formal declaration of allegiance to another State or given definite evidence of his determination to repudiate his allegiance to the State. Change of religion is not included in the category of recognised reasons for deprivation of nationality.[20] None of the Pakistan Constitutions of 1956, 1962 or 1973 contemplates such drastic action against a Muslim national, nor does the Pakistan Citizenship Act provide for such a contingency. Such a provision would be an indirect encroachment on the right of non-Muslim citizens to win over others to their own creed.

The creation of a veritable fifth column within the organised society, in the shape of hypocrites who have been coerced under the shadow of the sword to make a verbal but dishonest declaration of faith, would not redound to its security and stability. The dissident defector may have been assailed by genuine doubts and, unless he himself is persuaded to see the error of his thinking, how is he to be convinced where the truth lies? To each group of humans, as the Qur'an declares, its own creed is made to appear fair, and who but the Supreme Being should be the arbiter between truth and falsehood? That function He has reserved to Himself for decision on the Doomsday, and who are we to accelerate the Divine pace of requital for His disobedience in a field which is His preserve? To invest one group of human beings with the sole authority to decide such a question would lead to internecine warfare among organised communities. Providence has made this earthly sojourn a trial for us all and coercion or duress in this field would, as several exegetists of the Qur'an have declared, make the concept of trial meaningless.

---

20. S. Faruq A. Hasan, *Principles of Public International Law*, p. 135.

Moreover, the practice of the Prophet at Madīnah[21] in having a pact with the non-Muslims for certain State purposes and leaving them free to profess and follow their own religions, with equal political benefits to all parties, points to another alternative solution besides the two visualised by Mawlana Mawdudi. The question may well be posed: Is it possible to have a State peopled purely by persons professing a single faith? It will be shutting one's eyes to reality to imagine that a State, with the world system of today, could be set up with such exclusiveness.

Another big chink in the armour of those who uphold the orthodox view about the apostate's punishment is furnished by the exemption approved by the Ḥanafiyyah and the Imāmiyyah in favour of females and the reasons adduced in support of that exemption. A brief reference to that aspect of the problem has already been made earlier. Al-Sāmarā'ī has given a long extract from *Al-Mabsūṭ* of al-Sarakhsī in which he has referred to three *aḥādīth* according to which the Prophet disapproved of the killing of women on the ground that they do not possess the capacity to fight.[22] Al-Sarakhsī says in this context:

> And in this [the instances cited from the Prophet] there is specification that justification for killing is on the ground of *qitāl* (fighting) and women do not participate in fighting. In this respect there is no difference between original disbelief and adopted disbelief.

He then goes on to explain that the slaying is not requital for apostasy but that penalty is justified having regard to insistence on disbelief. This piece of subtle reasoning it would be difficult to accept. Further on, he expresses himself in these terms: "Change of faith and original disbelief are among the principal

---

21. Dr M. Hamidullah, *Siyāsī Wathīqah Jāt*: Urdu translation by M. Abu Yahya Imam Khan Nushihrawi, p. 19–24.
22. Al-Sāmarā'ī, *op. cit.*, pp. 219 *et seq*.

offences, but they are between the servant and his Lord." Consequently, their requital is postponed to the Hereafter. And what is hastened in this world by way of prescribed punishments is on account of interests that pertain to God's servants, like *qiṣāṣ* (penalty for murder) for the security of life; the punishment for fornication for protection of ancestry and the bed; the punishment for theft for the protection of property; the punishment for slander for the protection of honour and dignity; and the punishment for drinking for the preservation of the senses. By insistence on disbelief, a person wages war against the Muslims and so he is killed to remove the hostility. For God Almighty has expressly specified the ground for it at places, *eg.,* the verse: "If they fight you then slay them" (2:191). He makes explicit the cause that brings about the ground, at places, and that is association with God. So when it is established that the slaying is with reference to militancy, she will not be killed for original disbelief or for adopted disbelief, but will be imprisoned.

Similar opinions are recorded in the *Hidāyah* of Marghinānī, the *Fatḥ al-Qadīr* of Ibn Hammām, in al-Chalpī's gloss on the margin of *Fatḥ al-Qadīr*, in al-Ṭahāwī's *Kitāb al-Siyar* and in al-'Asqalānī's *Fatḥ al-Bārī*.[23] Mawlana Muhibbullah Bihari in his *Musallam al-Thabūt* offers an identical explanation for not killing a child if he apostatises after accepting Islam. He says he will only be imprisoned, for "killing is not for apostasy alone but for *ḥirābah* and he is incapable of it". He adds that he will not be punished even on attaining majority, for the validity of his initial acceptance of Islam is a subject of controversy among the learned, and this introduces an element of doubt into the situation.[24]

---

23. *Sharḥ Fatḥ al-Qadīr* (Ibn Hammām) *'alā al-Hidāyah Sharḥ Bidāyat al-Mubtadī* (Marghinānī) and on its margin *Sharḥ al-'Ināyah 'alā al-Hidāyah* (al-Bābartī) and comments of al-Chalpī, IV, 29. Ibn Ḥajar al-'Asqalānī, *Fatḥ al-Bārī*, XII, 33; Abū Ja'far al-Ṭahāwī, *Sharḥ Ma'ānī al-Āthār*, II, 34.
24. pp. 68–69.

If the true reason for slaying of an apostate is *muḥāribah* (active hostility or militancy), then the justification for the slaying of a peaceful male apostate who does not wish to give up his allegiance to the Islamic State would go by the board, on identical reasoning. This suggestion is not without respectable authority. Ibn Ḥayyān, in his *al-Baḥr al-Muḥīṭ*,[25] says in his commentary on the verse: "There is no compulsion in religion," that a person who forsakes Islam for another religion cannot be compelled to revert to Islam, according to one opinion, for this would destroy the concept of this phenomenal world being *dār al-ibtilā'* (house of trial) and a place wherein duties are imposed. This important pronouncement by an authority sufficiently important to be mentioned by Ibn Ḥayyān is in perfect harmony with the modern concepts of human organisation.

That *kufr* (disbelief) by itself does not justify shedding of blood and that only active hostility can provide the sanction for it, has been formulated as a basic principle by Shaykh Maḥmūd Shaltūt of Al-Azhar, in his *Al-Islām 'Aqīdah wa Sharī'ah*[26] and again in his *Tafsīr al-Qur'ān al-Karīm*[27] while interpreting Sūrah al-An'ām, verse 151: "And that you slay not the life that Allah has made sacred save in the course of justice." Al-Sāmarā'ī has also quoted the dictum in his *Aḥkām al-Murtadd*[28] and has further added that it is supported by what is said by Ibn Daqīq in *Iḥkām al-Aḥkām Sharḥ 'Umdat al-Aḥkām* and by al-Ṣan'ānī's opinion included in his *Al-'Iddah 'alā Iḥkām al-Aḥkām*. The extract from Ibn Daqīq's book, included in *Aḥkām al-Murtadd*, concerns the question whether a Muslim who does not offer prayers is to be killed or not. According to him, he cannot be

---

25. II, 281–282 (Riyadh ed.).
26. pp. 300–301.
27. p. 427.
28. pp. 114–115.

slain for this offence, unless he takes up arms against the Muslims on this issue. He then makes the following apt observations:

> There is difference between *muqātalah* (mutual fighting) over an issue and *qatl* (slaying) on its account. For *muqātalah* is mutual action which requires participation by two parties and from permission to fight over the issue of prayer, when fighting arises over it; it does not necessarily follow that it is permissible to slay a person not offering prayers, even when he does not fight over it.

Al-Ṣan'ānī, while agreeing with this opinion, cites the instance of persons who decline to pay *zakāh*. In such a case, he says, the *zakāh* will be taken from them by force and there will be no fighting and no killing, unless they initiate a fight, themselves.

The argument that a Muslim who has become an apostate deserves to be treated differently because he had received the call to the Truth, and had believed in it at one time, seems to be devoid of substance. If this theory has any merit, what would be said of non-Muslim scholars who have devoted a lifetime to the study of the Qur'an and the Islamic system of thought and action and have still adhered to their own faiths? Has not the call reached them and are they not offering an affront to the True Religion by their omission to accept Islam? The non-Muslim missionaries, some of whom invent all kinds of calumnies against Islam—should they not be held guilty of contempt of God's Word? If pushed to its extreme conclusion, this theory would involve Muslims in war with practically all disbelievers, within our country or without. Such an eventuality is not contemplated by the Qur'an or the *Sunnah* of the Prophet and it must be firmly held that the affront hypothesis has no rational basis. Neither authority nor reason would sanction the spirit of belligerency underlying this hypothesis. The myth that Islam was spread by the sword has been exploded by the writings of some of the fair-minded Western savants themselves. For illustration, one may refer to the scholarly work of Sir Thomas Arnold, *The Preaching of Islam*. Islam owes its success as a missionary religion to its freedom from irrational dogma and its principles of Divine Unity and human equality and fraternity which cut across the divisive factors of race, colour or geography, and the personal examples of service and piety on the part of devotees of the Faith. Some zealots may have overstepped the bounds of fair dealing, at times in our history, but these are exceptional occurrences of little significance in our collective ethos.

The enthusiasm for conformism has led some of our scholars to advocate the idea that an Islamic State cannot permit non-Muslims residing within its boundaries to propagate their own faith among Muslims, though they could allow them to do so among other non-Muslims and to teach their own children the tenets of their faith and, in the process, to subject the teachings of Islam also to balanced criticism.[29] This stance seems to be influenced by totalitarian ideas such as prevail under Fascist or Communist regimes and it may be humbly suggested that such a concept is not in keeping with the spirit of the Qur'an or the *Sunnah* of the Prophet. There is the classical instance of the Prophet allowing the Christian delegation from Najrān to stay in his own mosque and to perform their worship rites therein. He debated the questions pertaining to the Faith with them and when he found them to be impervious to rational argument, he challenged them to *mubāhalah* (mutual invocation of the Curse of God on the ground that takes a false stand), but the Christians sought shy of it. He did not bar their right to advocate the truth

---

29. M. Abul A'la Mawdudi, *op. cit.*, pp. 32–39, 77.

of their own creed. Islam must stand on the excellence of its own teachings and needs no protective shield against exchange of views at the intellectual level. Indeed a missionary religion like Islam must be prepared for discussion of the relative merits of various religious beliefs, in the field of comparative study, before it can hope to convince others of its own superiority, of course within the bounds of decency and decorum.

A careful study of the fundamentals of our religion and our history can fairly lead to the inference that apostasy alone, unalloyed by hostility to the established order, is not amenable to the disciplining dictates of any human tribunal, but that punishment for an offence of this nature must be left to the All-Wise Creator Himself. The instances in which apostates forfeited their lives in the lifetime of the the Prophet or during the regime of the Rightly-Guided Caliphs do not justify a general rule that a non militant apostate must be put to death. In most of these cases there was superadded to the change of faith an element of rebellion against the State or hostility to the Muslims. In those days, it was, in all probability, a legitimate presumption to make that a person forsaking the Islamic fold would join the ranks of enemies of the Muslims, and history seems to bear out this presumption. Consequently in the writings of the old jurists, the distinction between apostasy simpliciter and active hostility to the community came to be blurred and, in the course of time, the presumption hardened into the rule that an apostate, unless he repents, must be condemned to death.

The historical incidents involving such condemnation can be very appropriately referred to the principle of *ta'zīr* a— punishment devised by the sovereign authority, as an expedient step to safeguard the collective interest, in the circumstances prevailing at the relevant times. For such disciplinary measures, the government principle is thus stated by Dr 'Abd al-Ḥamīd al-Mutawallī, Professor, Law Faculty, Alexandria, University of Egypt in his *Mabādī' Niẓām al-Ḥukm fī al-Islām*[30]:

> It must be noted that those who talk of apostasy being an offence entailing the death sentence do not class it as among the *jarā'im al-ḥudūd* (offences which invite punishment prescribed in the Qur'an). For apostasy is categorised by the learned as among *al-jarā'im al-ta'zīriyyah* (offences which attract *ta'zīr*—punishment emanating from the competent authority), and it is known that there is an important distinction between *jarā'im al-ḥudūd* and *al-jarā'im al-ta'zīriyyah*. The distinction lies in this that punishment in the case of *ta'zīriyyah* offences is not determined (that is, fixed beforehand) as contrasted with the cases of offences inviting *ḥudūd*. The preferred opinion among the *fuqahā'* is that the determination of punishment for *ta'zīriyyah* offences is left to (the discretion of) the person in authority (to one who has the authority to pass judgement), and it follows that he can fix any of the punishments except for the sentence of death, in conformity with what would suit the circumstances of the community. And for a long time, this matter has been relegated to determination by the person in authority. Thus there is no obligation to fix a punishment for an action if the collective interest does not require its determination.

The upshot of the discussion is that the *fuqahā'*, though seemingly upholding an almost agreed doctrine of death for apostasy, yet reveal a variety of opinions as to the rationale of such punishment. They, directly or indirectly, all accept that active hostility is the real justification for harshness to apostates. Basing themselves, as they do, on historical instances which involved such hostility to the community, they felt no necessity to differentiate between peaceful conversions to other faiths and violent defections. Some old as well as modern jurists have taken

---

30. pp. 747–748 (1st ed.).

pains to clarify that disbelief, whether original or adopted, does not justify the shedding of blood, and this clearly *per se* creates a dichotomy in their thinking. On the one hand, they prescribe the extreme penalty for apostasy and on the other affirm the principle that disbelief *per se* is not punishable. It is difficult to reconcile these two views on the logical plane.

There is also a parallel strain of human compassion and understanding, based on the Word of God, clearly discernible in the writings of those who would allow a whole lifetime for repentance to the renegade, which practically means the negation of any punishment for apostasy. The result thus arrived at, by an indirect route, accords well with the Divine Dispensation, and further strengthens the inference that a peaceful conversion of a Muslim to another faith is not actionable.

CHATTER V

Ijtihād and *Ijmā'*

Conservative scholars often set up the bar of *ijmā* (consensus) against the reopening of a question, even if the exigencies of time and place require its reexamination. Thus, while paying lip service to the principle of *ijtihād*, they shut out, in practice, all fresh thinking on the individual or group level on any matter which they regard as settled by a previous consents. The punishment for apostasy is also said to fall in this closed category. It is, therefore, necessary to examine how far this claim has validity under Islamic Law.

The classical legal theory of Islamic *fiqh* envisages four basic sources of Islamic Law—the Qur'an, the *Sunnah* of the Prophet, *Ijmā'* (consensus) and *Qiyās* (analogical deduction). Importance attaches to these sources according to their sequence in this ordered scheme. There can be little doubts, however, that the concept of *ijmā'*, more particularly the *ijmā'* of the Prophet's Companions, emerged in the course of historical evolution, most probably after the first generation had passed away. Dr Ahmad Hasan, Reader, Islamic Research Institute Islamabad, has pointed out that the jurists of the old school placed *qiyās* before *ijmā'*, as is borne out by the record of discussions Imām al-Shāfi'ī had with his opponents. The change in the order of precedence of the sources appears first in al-Shāfi'ī, though the ground for the change appears to have been laid earlier. As the learned scholar aptly remarks, *ijmā'* can emerge only out of a diversity of opinions expressed at the level of individual *qiyās* through a process of gradual integration. *Qiyās* and *ijmā'* thus complement each other in a continuous process, during which the Qur'an and the *Sunnah* continue to occupy the position of being the basic material sources of Islamic Law.[1]

It is curious that the definition of *ijmā'* itself has varied from time to time in classical *fiqh* literature. Two earlier definitions that "*ijmā'* is an agreement of the Islamic community on a religious point" and "*ijmā'* is a consensus of opinion of the *Ahl al-Ijmā'* (those competent for *ijmā'*) when a religious issue arises, whether rational or legal," were abandoned as unsound by later jurists. The accepted standard definition appears to be that "*ijmā'* is a unanimous agreement of the jurists of the community, of a particular era, on a certain issue." As Dr Ahmad Hasan rightly observes, this too is a theoretical definition and does not represent the actual historical process of *ijmā'* in Islam. For, according to the classical theory, it is not complete if even one person competent for *ijtihād* (interpretation) and *naẓar* (insight) remains opposed to the agreed decision. Such a total *ijmā'* "is not a practicable proposition". After detailed analysis of several instances in which *ijmā'* was supposed to conclude the view pressed, the learned scholar finds that *ijmā'* various provinces of the early Islamic State meant only the average opinion of the lawyers of each province, and not the universal *ijmā'* of all regions.[2]

Dr Fazlur Rahman, a well known scholar and ex-Director, Islamic Research Institute, Islamabad, has highlighted al-Shāfi'ī's position, on the authority of his *Kitāb al-Umm,* by observing that

---

1. Ahmad Hasan, *The Early Development of Islamic Jurisprudence*, pp. 40–42.
2. *Ibid.*, p 155.

he ceaselessly agreed against the claims of his opponents—the representatives of the older schools—to have arrived at a state of general *ijmā*'; that, apart from certain basic facts like the number of prayers, etc., in fact, not *ijmā*' but difference prevailed on almost all issues and that no formal council of Muslim representatives, to reach agreements, had ever been convened nor was such a step feasible.[3]

Again, we have it from that eminent savant, M. Charagh 'Ali (Nawāb A'ẓam Yar Jung) that Shaykh Muḥyī al-Dīn ibn al-'Arabī, Dāwūd al-Ẓāhirī, Ibn Ḥabbān, Ibn Ḥazm and, according to one report, Imām Aḥmad bin Ḥanbal, rejected all *ijmā*' as non-authentic except for the *ijmā*' of the Prophet's Companions; that Naẓẓām and, according to another report, Imām Aḥmad bin Ḥanbal denied the validity of all *ijmā*' and that Imām Mālik pinned his faith to the *ijmā*' of the residents of Madīnah alone.[4] To this may be added that the Imāmiyyah recognise only the agreement of members of the Prophet's family. It may, therefore, be said with some justification that no consensus exists on the definition of *ijmā*'.

Mawlana Muhammad Hanif Nadvi of Lahore assigns only a corroborative role to *ijmā*' and does not regard it as possessing a creative or positive authority, leading to any new juristic reality. He clarifies that there is no agreed decision on any issue whose validity might have been established by *ijmā*' alone and regarding which no persuasive argument may be available from the Qur'an and *Sunnah*. He distinctly visualises that a departure from *ijmā*' may, on occasions, turn out to be sound and healthy. He cites the instance of Ibn Taymiyyah disagreeing with the accepted view based on a ruling of 'Umar, the Second Caliph, that three *ṭalāqs* (divorces) pronounced in one sitting constitute *ṭalāq*

---

3. Fazlur Rahman, *Islamic Methodology in History*, pp. 21-22.
4. Charagh 'Ali, *A 'ẓam al-Kalām fī Irtiqā' al-Islām*, pp. 21-22.

bā'in (irrevocable divorce) and observes sagely that a dispassionate consideration of the arguments advanced on either side would lead to the conclusion that the truth is with Ibn Taymiyyah and *ijmā'* with the revered jurists of the four orthodox *Sunnī* schools. His verdict is that so long as liberty to resort to *ijtihād* and *qiyās* on the basis of the Qur'an and *Sunnah* and variation in the complexion of a problem due to changed circumstances exists, on *ijmā'* can bar recourse to *qiyās* and *ijtihād*.[5]

Some jurists rely on the Qur'anic verses 3:103 and 4:115, for supporting the validity of *ijmā'*. Dr Ahmad Hasan has, in this context, commented on the lack of all evidence that these verses, which are of a general character, were understood in the sense claimed, during the time of the Prophet and his Companions.[6] Similarly, in respect of the oft-quoted *ḥadīth*: "My community will never agree on an error," the opinion of Shah Waliyullah is very illuminating that this only means that there will always be some people who would remain on the straight path and the community, therefore, will not agree on error.[7]

That an earlier collective opinion, if one exists, can be superseded by a later one, is a proposition which finds mention in Imām al-Ghazālī's *Fayṣal al-Tafriqah bayn al-Islām wa al-Zandaqah*, as was noted by Sir Sayyid Ahmad Khan while summarising its contents in an essay.[8] The eminent modern scholar, Dr Muhammad Hamidullah, has expressed a similar opinion on the authority of al-Bukhārī's *Kashf al-Asrār 'Alā Uṣūl al-Bazdawī*.[9]

In the course of a discussion on the distinction between *ḥadd*

---

5. M. Hanif Nadwi, *Mas'alah-i Ijtihād*, pp. 103–04.
6. *op. cit.*, pp. 15–59.
7. Shah Waliyullah, *Ḥujjat Allāh al-Bālighah* (Urdu translation), II, 61–62.
8. *Maqālāt-i Sir Sayyid*, III, 109 and 166.
9. See his article on Jurisprudence in M.M. Sharif, Ed., *A History of Muslim Philosophy*, II, 1230.

(prescribed punishment) and *ta'zīr* (undetermined punishment left within the discretion of those in authority), Mawlana Muhammad Taqi Amini refers to al-Marghinānī's opinion in the *Hidāyah* that all punishments fixed by the Qur'an, the *Sunnah* and *ijmā'* are included in the definition of *ḥadd*. He further notes that al-Māwardī defines this term as comprehending those punishments which God Almighty has prescribed in order to deter persons from committing prohibited acts or omitting obligatory ones, but he, too, in his subsequent exposition, includes within its purview punishment for omissions like abstinence from prayer, for which the Qur'an specifies no punishment in this world. This is a confusing state of affairs and the learned scholar rightly suggests that, in the interest of clarity, the scope of *ḥudūd* should be confined to Qur'anic prescriptions and all other punishments should be classified under the category of *ta'zīr*. He then observes that there may be some *ta'zīrī* crimes for which punishments may have been prescribed during the regime of the first four Caliphs, and for which the claim of finality may be made on account of previous consensus. But, according to him, changed circumstances would justify their revision, within the framework of *nuṣūṣ* (explicit texts).[10]

'Allāmah Iqbal has discussed the incidents of *ijtihād* and *ijmā'* in his sixth lecture. On the point of *ijtihād* he says:

> The closing of the door of *ijtihād* is pure fiction suggested partly by the crystallisation of legal thought in Islam, and partly by that intellectual laziness which, especially in the period of spiritual decay, turns great thinkers into idols.[11]

In respect of a consensus of the Companions, the 'Allāmah has made the following pertinent observations:

---

10. Muhammad Taqi Amini, *Ahkām-i Shar'iyyah min Ḥalāt wa Zamānah kī Ri'āyat*, pp. 93–94.
11. *The Reconstruction of Religious Thoughts in Islam*, p. 178.

I think it is necessary in this connexion to discriminate between a decision relating to a question of fact and the one relating to a question of law. In the former case, as for instance, when the question arose whether the two small *Sūrahs* known as '*al-Mu'awwidhatain*' formed part of the Qur'an or not, and the companions unanimously decided that they did, we are bound by their decision, obviously because the companions alone were in a position to know the fact. In the latter case the question is one of interpretation only, and I venture to think, on the authority of Karkhī, that later generations are not bound by the decision of the companions. Says Karkhī: "The *Sunnah* of the companions is binding in matters which cannot be cleared up by *Qiyās*, but it is not so in matters which can be established by *Qiyās*.[12]

This being the history and legal position of *ijmā'*, there seems very little force in the assertion that the possibility of *ijtihād* in the field covered by a previous consensus, if such indeed exists, is foreclosed for ever. Of course the institution of *ijmā'*, when fully developed, may serve to bring order into the chaos of conflicting opinion and may be utilised to transfer the power of *ijtihād* from individual representatives of schools to a Muslim legislative assembly, as 'Allāmah Iqbal has suggested.[13] But this does not mean that individual *qiyās* should be forbidden after a matter has been decided by a consensus of a Muslim assembly. Later socio-political developments may justify a fresh assessment of a problem and in such a case the initiative should remain with all thinking individuals who may feel the call to draw the attention of the community to the desirability of a fresh orientation. If every consensus, when arrived at, is to become sacrosanct, it would, eventually, stifle all intellectual debate at the individual or communal level and lead to stagnation of the community in a changing world.

---

12. *Ibid.*, p. 175.
13. *Ibid.*, pp. 173–174.

Typical among scholars who stand for the inviolability of *ijmā'* is the head of the Jamā'at-i Islāmī, M. Abul A'la Mawdudi. The Mawlana has briefly touched this point in his interview published in the daily *Nawā'-i Waqt* of 7 June 1973, but he has expatiated on it, at some length, in his article reproduced in an issue of the same daily dated 28 July 1973. Therein he has asserted in the beginning of his article that a consensus once arrived at cannot be undone by any subsequent intellectual exercise. He has pronounced this verdict specifically in the context of the supposed consensus on the prescribed punishment for apostasy being death.

In the first place it may be doubted if such a consensus on the question under examination, in fact, exists. It has been brought out elsewhere in this book that at least one contrary opinion among the old *fuqahā'* has received prominent mention in the celebrated *tafsīr*, *Al-Bahr al-Muhīt* and that has been the subject of an explanatory gloss from Abū Muslim and Qifāl. But it appears that the Mawlana's claim is vitiated by an inconsistency in his own writing, of which he does not seem to be conscious. While summarising the legal position in the last paragraph of his above-mentioned article, he has said:

> According to the Hanafī school, apostate women have been permanently exempted from the extreme penalty. Ibrāhīm al-Nakha'ī believes in allowing unlimited opportunity for repentance to an apostate. Similar other instances are to be found among the various schools of *Fiqh*, which go to establish that to regard death as the sole punishment for apostasy is an erroneous idea.

It may be pointed out, with respect, that the claim in the earlier part of the article, that *ijmā'* had finally settled the death sentence for an apostate, has evaporated into thin air, by the time the Mawlana approached the end of his article.

The trend of enlightened opinion in recent times favours the thesis that apostasy is not punishable unless allied with an attempt at socio-political subversion. In Chapter IV, the opinion of a modern Egyptian scholar, Dr 'Abd al-Ḥamīd Mutawallī, has already been sent out in this context. The venerable *Ahl al-Ḥadīth* scholar, M. Thana'ullah of Amritsar, in his book *Islām aur Masīḥiyyat* has referred to verse 137 of Sūrah al-Nisā' ("Those who believe, then disbelieve and then again believe, then disbelieve and thereafter increase in disbelief, Allah will never pardon them nor will He guide them into a way") and to two *aḥādīth* generally relied upon to support the death sentence for an apostate and has formulated his final opinion on this question in these words:

> Thus if the *ḥadīth* [the Mawlana is referring to the combined effect of the two *aḥādīth*] is read with the Qur'an, the conclusion clearly emerges that *irtidād* alone does not justify slaying (of the apostate). *irtidād* calls for the death sentence only in a case where the apostate joins the enemy ranks out of ill-will towards Muslims. Today, under Military Law, a soldier is court-martialled for very ordinary transgressions and this course is justified by necessity. So it must be held that in the relevant *ḥadīth*, military law has been enunciated, which is being acted upon by the world today ... Therefore, it is unjustified to accuse Islam of denying liberty of conscience on the basis of such military law, for each subtle point has its appropriate place.

To similar effect are the forceful observations of the celebrated scholar, M. Charagh 'Ali (Nawab A'zam Yar Jung).[14]

As has been mentioned earlier, the late Mawlana Muhammad 'Ali Jawhar had taken up cudgels, on behalf of the progressive group, against the orthodox section, in 1924–1925 and had sponsored the thesis that neither authority nor reason required the

---

14. *op. cit.*, pp. 89–94.

apostate to be put to death unless he was additionally guilty of waging war against the State or established society. He was accused of siding with the scholars of the Aḥmadiyyah sect in this connection, but that did not deter him from a free and frank expression of his well-considered views, for which he quoted chapter and verse from the Qur'an and *Sunnah*.

The *Payghām-i Ṣulḥ*, a paper published by the Lahore Aḥmadiyyah section, supplies useful information on the views expressed, in those days, by some other non-Aḥmadī savants on the point in controversy. It appears that the Honourable Sir Raza 'Ali, Mawlana M. Isma'il Ghaznawi of Amritsar, Mawlawi Sayyid Mumtaz 'Ali, Editor, *Tahdhībi Niswān*, Lahore, the well-known leader, Dr. Sayf al-Din Kitchlew, S. Maqbul Aḥmad, Deputy Collector, Allahabad (who claimed to have made an extensive study of the Arabic language and Islamic *fiqh*), 'Allāmah Abu al-Fadl Ahsanullah 'Abbasi and the venerable scholar, M. Aslam Jairajpuri had ranged themselves on the progressive side, in this controversy. The last-named savant's well-reasoned article had appeared in the magazine *Jāmi'ah* of Aligarh and the *Payghām-i Ṣulḥ* reproduced it *in extenso*. The learned scholar, after citing several Qur'anic verses had, *inter alia*, maintained that it is the duty of Muslims even to go to war to suppress religious persecution; and, therefore, for Muslims to resort to coercion to keep an erring Muslim within the fold of Islam would mean worshipping the very idol which they were commanded to destroy. After considering the relevant to Qur'anic verses and the *aḥādīth*, he clearly enunciated the opinion that the latter covered cases of political offenders rather than religious delinquents and that they really fell within the purview of verse 33 of Sūrah al-Mā'idah.[15]

---

15. *Payghām-i Ṣulḥ*, issues dated 2 November, 9 November, 16 November, 23 November 1924, 14 January, 1 March, 4 March, 11 March and 13 December 1925.

Mawlana Muhammad Taqi Amini, Director, Religious Studies, Muslim University, Aligarh, has expressed identical views on the question.[16]

Both Mawlana Muhammad Hanif Nadvi, Deputy Director, Institute of Islamic Culture, Lahore, and 'Allāmah Alauddin Siddiqi, ex-Vice-Chancellor, University of the Punjab, were interviewed by a special correspondent of the daily *Nawā'-i Waqt*, on 7 June 1973 and their views, as published in that paper's issue of the same date, are in no way different from the thesis developed in the present book.

Professor Qamar al-Din Khan, Fellow, Islamic Research Institute, Islamabad, writing under the caption "Freedom of Conscience in Muslim Society," in *The Pakistan Times* dated 18 November 1973, has aptly observed that a religion that aspires to live by compulsion and coercion cannot live long and, therefore, the freedom to believe must be equated with the freedom to disbelieve. "A careful study of history," he says, "would reveal that punishments to renegades were always motivated by political reasons."

The late Mufti 'Abd al-Qayyum, an advocate of Lahore, was a profound scholar of Muslim *fiqh* and author of several books on Islamic subjects. The author had the benefit of a discussion with him, in his lifetime, on the theme of the present book and he was good enough to put down his views in writing for me. He was in full accord with the thesis developed in this book.

Two scholars had the occasion to review the first edition of this book—the late Dr Wahid Mirza, one time editor of the *Urdu Encyclopaedia of Islam* and Mr Rafī'allah Shihab, Lecturer, Government College, Gujar Khan, and both fully endorsed the views expressed herein. The former's review appeared in *The*

---

16. *op. cit.*, pp. 127–128, 181, 188.

Pakistan Times dated 10 December 1973 and the latter's learned article (in which he also dealt with the criticism of this book by Mr 'Abd al-Hamid Siddiqi, Editor, *Tarjumān al-Qur'ān*, Lahore) was published in the *Ṭulū'ī Islām*, Lahore, of December 1973. I also recall with gratification that I received an appreciative letter from another scholar, Sayyid Ya'qub Shah, Retired Auditor General of Pakistan. The learned Editor of the *Ṭulū'ī Islām*, Mr Ghulam Ahmad Pervaiz, had already controverted Mawlana Mawdudi's views on this subject, in his book *Qatli Murtadd, Ghulān aur aundiyān*.

'Allāmah Iqbal, as far as I am aware, had no occasion to examine the issue herein discussed in all its juristic bearings, but in his "Reply to Questions Raised by Pundit Jawaharlal Nehru," he has made the following pertinent observations:

> It is true that when a person, declared to be holding heretical doctrines, threatens the existing social order, an independent Muslim State will certainly take action, but, in such a case, the action of the State will be determined more by political consideration than by purely religious one.[17]

This would tend to the inference that the 'Allāmah, at best, regarded the punishment of an apostate as a *ta'zīr* and not as a *ḥadd*.

An article from the pen of Mawlana Muhammad Ja'far Phulwarwi appeared in *Al-Ma'ārif* of Lahore, in April 1976. On the authority of verses 86–90 of Sūrah Āl 'Imrān, the learned scholar has declared unequivocally that an apostate is not punishable with death for his apostasy alone. If an intending apostate simulates the role of a Muslim, under threat of death, to save his skin, the result would be hypocrisy and not adherence to the true Faith. No one who believes in "There is no compulsion

---

17. S.A. Wahid, Ed., *Thoughts and Reflections of Iqbal*, p. 263.

in religion" can, according to the Mawlana approve of such a thing. He adds that the historical instances in which apparently apostates were given the capital punishment were really cases of rebellion.

I am sure there must be other scholars in the country, unknown to me, holding similar progressive views. I earnestly hope that what has been said above will suffice as evidence of the leaven of fresh thinking working in the community such as may culminate in due course in a fresh consensus, in the changed global conditions of today. May the All-Knowing Allah guide us aright in all our affairs!

CHAPTER VI

Summary and Conclusions

The Qur'an gives us in unambiguous terms the fundamentals of the Islamic faith and sets out the basic principles which should govern an Islamic polity. A principle that stands out conspicuously in the sociopolitical dispensation of the Book of God is epitomised in the noble words: "There is no compulsion in religion." This principle finds endorsement in several other verses of the Qur'an, which manifestly tolerate, though they disapprove of, divergences from the Straight Path. The highest value is attached to the condition of the mind and heart of a person as compared to lip service to the ideals of good life, and the test of right-mindedness is to be manifested in deeds and not mere words. Man is free to choose between truth and falsehood and the Prophet's function is to convey the message, exemplify it in his own life and to leave the rest to God—he is no warder over men to compel them to adopt particular beliefs. Liberty of conscience is thus a value of the good life itself and must be kept in view when studying the incidents and effect of *aḥādīth*, the practice during the Rightly-Guided Caliphate or the opinions of Doctors of Law which must not depart from the letter or the spirit of God's Word. The fountainhead of wisdom and guidance is the Qur'an, and the injunctions contained therein must be accorded a status akin to that of a fundamental constitutional law, in the light of which all affairs in the sociopolitical field are to be regulated and interpreted.

Our study of the relevant Qur'anic verses establishes that the punishment for apostasy is postponed to the Hereinafter, in the same way as that for original disbelief. There is absolutely no mention in the Qur'an of mundane punishment for defection from the Faith by a believer, except in the shape of deprivation of the spiritual benefits of Islam or of the civil status and advantages that accrue to an individual as a member of the well-knit fraternity of Muslims. He should, however, be free to profess and propagate the faith of his choice, so long as he keeps within the bounds of law and morality, and to enjoy all other rights as a peaceful citizen of the State, in common with his Muslim co-citizens. Not only is there no specific provision in the Qur'an, prescribing punishment for an apostate in the phenomenal world, but several verses of the Holy Book envisage the natural death of the apostate in his condition of disbelief and even contemplate repeated apostasies and reversions to the true Faith, on the part of an individual. He has also his whole lifetime available to him for repentance, short of the actual moment of death.

This position positively militates against the theory evolved in the course of our religious history that an apostate must receive the capital sentence, immediately or after a short period of grace, on his very first defection. The Qur'an, however, permits fighting and the severest action against those who are actively hostile to the Muslim community or seek to disrupt the social order but only till such time as peace is restored, and it is ensured that religion is for Allah only, which means that all religious persecution should cease.

A survey of the relevant incidents that occurred in the Holy Prophet's lifetime reveals no departure from the Divine norms, and this indeed was to be eminently expected of the Perfect Exemplar. Some reported sayings of the Prophet, which appeared to be couched in general terms and whose circumstantial antecedents are not clearly known, must receive specific interpretations such as would involve factual presumptions for bringing them into conformity with the words of the Qur'an. The possibility that the narrators who have transmitted these sayings had omitted to give, of failed to recollect, the appurtenant circumstances cannot be excluded. In the case of some of these sayings, a few qualifications have been read into them by our Doctors of Law themselves and our suggested presumptions are, therefore, not without warrant, specially when the overriding consideration is kept in mind that no action or saying of the Prophet could have been contradictory to what is explicitly mentioned in the Qur'an. Indeed some positive instances in which the Prophet of God refrained from action against apostates have been found to exist, and this fortifies the suggested assumptions underlying the reported general sayings. In the face of such instances, it is difficult to postulate that the Prophet had enunciated a general rule prescribing the death penalty for apostasy simpliciter.

The occurrences during the regimes of the four Rightly-Guided Caliphs, on which the thesis of the capital punishment for apostasy partly rests, have also been examined, and the inference emerges that they were illustrations of requital for active hostility or social disruption and not merely for peaceful dissent from the true Faith, after its initial acceptance. In some of these cases, the relevant facts are shrouded in obscurity so that no clear guidance is furnished by them. Verbal utterances of some of the Caliphs, bearing on the subject, which seem to suggest a general and rigorous rule that apostasy must be visited with the death sentence, in the absence of full knowledge of the facts to which they pertained, would require to be interpreted in consonance with the letter and spirit of the Qur'an, and the assumption would be legitimate that the persons concerned had committed not merely *lèse-majesté* of the Faith but that they had also transgressed the limits of civic liberty, to the prejudice of the collective interests of the community. Some of theses sayings are of dubious authenticity. Moreover, no opinion based on individual *ijtihād* of even an august *Ṣaḥābī* can be accepted as a binding precedent, if it is found to be contrary to the Divine injunctions or the Prophet's practice, directly or indirectly. Some instances indeed, in which the extreme penalty was withheld from an apostate, fortify the conclusion that no inelastic general rule on the subject existed and each case was conditioned by its exigencies.

The *fuqahā'* (jurists) acknowledge generally that no punishment for apostasy is expressly prescribed in the Qur'an. Their principal reliance for the view that apostasy must he punished with death is on certain *qawlī* (verbal) *aḥādīth*, but as has been brought out in the discussion of those sayings, the relevant occasion or the circumstances to which they might have reference are not fully explained. Some of these sayings have been subjected to qualifications and exceptions by some very acute minds among the jurisconsults, and it is only a justifiable further step that a presumption about their factual basis being *ḥirāb* or *muḥāribah* (active hostility to the community) should be raised. The attempt to gain indirect support from some verses of the Qur'an for the orthodox view cannot be described as successful. Historically speaking, the defectors from the Faith, in olden times, almost invariably joined the enemy ranks and became violent antagonists of Muslims. That seems to be the genesis of the prescription of the capital sentence for apostasy and no necessity was apparently felt of analyzing the circumstances of each individual case to discover whether the element of *ḥirāb* co-existed with apostasy or not. In course of time, decisions justifiable on their own facts hardened into a general rule prescribing the extreme penalty for apostasy. At least one old exgetist, Abī Ḥayyān al-Andalūsī sets out an opinion that even an apostate cannot be coerced into reversion to the Faith. Apparently he regarded this opinion as important enough to be mentioned in his well-known *tafsīr, Al-Baḥr al-Muḥīṭ*. Some of the jurists have adopted positions which reveal a conflict between their dicta on the logical plane. While adopting the generally held view that apostasy is punishable with death, they at the same time commit themselves to the principle that the shedding of blood is not requital for apostasy *per se*, but that the real ground is *muḥāribah* against Muslims. Notable figures in this category are al-Chalpī, Ibn Hammām and Muḥibbullah Bihārī among older jurists and Shaykh Maḥmūd Shaltūt, a modern Egyptian scholar. From this dictum, the next logical step would be to postulate that a peaceful apostasy is not punishable but that the apostate would be liable to punishment only if he takes up arms against the community or otherwise attempts to disrupt the social order. The view of some jurists that apostasy itself amounts to *muḥāribah* is contradicted by others and cannot be justified on any rational ground.

Indirect support is lent to these dissentient voices by a different line of approach favoured by some of the old Doctors of Law. In contrast with the majority view that either no opportunity for repentance should be allowed to a renegade or that only a limited period of grace would be permissible, Ibrāhīm al-Nakha'ī and Sufyān al-Thawrī held the opinion that the door of repentance was always open to a defector from the Faith during his lifetime and that clearly implies, as Ibn Qudāmah has observed while commenting on this opinion, that an apostate can never be killed. This position, it is submitted, is much more in harmony with the Qur'anic texts than the generally accepted orthodox view that a change of faith by a Muslim invites the penalty of death. Some of the exegetists of the Qur'an have made it absolutely clear that on the basis of God's Word, the choice of one's faith must be a voluntary act, unfettered by pressure or coercion of any kind and that any other view would negative God's scheme of this earthly life being an ordeal and an opportunity for testing the individual soul's capacity for righteousness, in the empirical terrestrial setting. It this respect no rational distinction can be made between original and adopted disbelief. The argument based on supposed indignity offered to Islam by a renegade should be set against the consideration that it would be much more undignified for the true Faith to retain adherents by coercion. By and large the orthodox dictum is sought to be buttressed with questionable logic and reasoning that is unconscious of its own inner contradictions.

At best, punishment for apostasy can be adopted by way of *ta'zīr* and not as a *ḥadd* specified in the Qur'an. The position would be analogous to breaking a prohibition, for example, with regard to drinking, for which the Qur'an does not expressly prescribe a definite punishment. The principle of *ta'zīr* is that both the propriety and measures of punishment for such offences which require to be suppressed in the collective interest, at any particular time or in a particular exigency, depends on the discretion of the sovereign authority. A relevant consideration, however, would be that apostasy being an offence in the realm of the rights of God (*ḥuqūq Allāh*) rather than the rights of mankind (*ḥuqūq al-'Ibād*), as al-Sarakhsī has pointed out, may well be left to be dealt with by the Almighty in the Hereafter and there would be no pressing necessity to punish a peaceful defection from the Faith. It would be expedient not to punish such a peaceful change of faith, for fear of reprisals by other non-Islamic States and to avoid the danger of internecine wars between organised communities. This course is also consistent with the doors of missionary activity of Muslims being kept open.

In this context, it maybe appropriate to remember that Pakistan is a member of the United Nations whose Charter declares in its Preamble that the Peoples of the United Nations are determined, *inter alia*, to reaffirm faith in fundamental human rights and in the dignity and worth of the human person. Article 1 of that Charter lays it down as one of the purposes of the United Nations

> to achieve international co-operation in solving international problems of an economic, social, cultural or humanitarian character and promoting and encouraging respect for human rights and for fundamental freedoms for all, without distinction as to race, sex, language or religion.

Article 55 of the Charter prescribes that "with a view to the creation of conditions of stability and well-being which are necessary for peaceful and friendly relations among nations, based on respect for the principle of equal rights and self-determination of people, the United Nations shall promote:

> … (c) Universal respect for and observance of human rights and fundamental freedoms for all, without distinction as to race, sex, language or religion.

Article 56 provides that:

> All members pledge themselves to take joint and separate action in co-operation with the Organisation for the achievement of the purposes set forth in Article 55.

On 10 December 1948, the General Assembly of the United Nations passed and proclaimed the "Universal Declaration of Human Rights". Article 18 of that Declaration reads as follows:

Everyone has the right to freedom of thought, conscience and religion; this right includes freedom to change his religion or belief and freedom, either alone or in community with others and in public or private, to manifest his religion or belief in teaching, practice, worship and observance.

The Declaration may not, in law, amount to a binding agreement among the nations, but it represents by consensus the common aspirations of the world community and at least places a moral obligation on members of the United Nations not to disregard its provisions. It may be added that these provisions do not appear to be repugnant to the liberal spirit of tolerance of the Qur'an and the *Sunnah* and there is consequently no reason for refusal to abide by them. It was probably in recognition, partly, of this salient fact that the Constitutions of 1956, 1962 and 1973 promulgated in Pakistan guaranteed to all citizens, including the minority communities, equality before the Law, equal protection of the Law and the right to profess, practice and propagate any religion, subject to law, public order and morality. The Fundamental Rights assured to citizens in these constitutional instruments also included the right of any religious denomination to establish, maintain and manage its own religious institutions and the right of any citizens to preserve its own distinctive culture. These rights were declared to be justiciable and the framers of these three Constitutions were obviously conscious of the international understanding on the subject.

But coming nearer home, we come across a more fundamental fact. Ch. Muhammad 'Ali, an ex-Prime Minister of Pakistan in his book, *The Emergence of Pakistan* (p. 240), while commenting on the Qā'id-i A'ẓam's first address to the Constituent Assembly of Pakistan, delivered on 11 August 1947, has made the following observations:

What is overlooked is that Pakistan came into existence not by conquest but as the result of a negotiated agreement between the representatives of the Hindu and Muslim communities to partition the subcontinent. An explicit and integral part of the agreement was that the minorities in both states would have equal rights and equal protection of law. In that context, the Qā'id-i A'ẓam was wholly right in asserting the fundamental principle that "we are all citizens of one State". It follows that the state must give full protection to religious beliefs of its subjects [and] should wholly and solely concentrate on the well-being of people and especially of the masses and the poor". These practical tasks of statesman-ship can be fulfilled only by giving equal rights and equal respon-sibilities to all citizens. But this can neither negate the fact that vast majority of the citizens of Pakistan are Muslims, nor take away the responsibilities for leadership from the Muslim community. The principles of governing the country will inevitably be based on Islam, if the leadership is sincere in its professions ...

These agreed guarantees, in effect, give the status of *mu'āhids* (people with whom there is a pact) to non-Muslims who live in Pakistan and owe allegiance to the Islamic State under the auspices of the Constitution. One may hazard the prediction, without much fear of contradiction, that a similar pattern of guaranteed fundamental rights would also form part of any future constitution of this country. In these circumstances, there would be a distinct impediment in the way of our legislators, if a proposal is put forward to make apostasy on the part of a Muslim to be punishable under any law enforceable in our Courts. The persons in authority would be constrained, in consequence, to exercise their discretion, against such legislation and no punishment even by way of *ta'zīr* would be regarded as apt for defection from the Faith. In the humble opinion of the present writer, such a consummation would be in conformity with the Qur'anic texts which remove punishment for disbelief, whether original or adopted, from the purview of the short span of human life on this earth and relegate it to the eternal life after death. The august practice of the Prophet of Islam is in no sense in conflict with this position.

Bibliography

Commentaries of the Qur'an

Aḥkām al-Qur'ān—Abī Bakr Aḥmad bin 'Alī al-Rāzī al-Jaṣṣāṣ (Maṭba'at al-Bihīyyat al-Miṣriyyah, 1347 H.).

Aḥkām al-Qur'ān—Abī Bakr Muḥammad bin 'Abdullah known as Ibn al-'Arabī (1st ed., 1367/1957).

Anwār al-Tanzīl wa Asrār al-Ta'wīl—Nāṣir al-Dīn 'Abdullah bin 'Umar bin Muḥammad al-Bayḍāwī, with *Tafsīr al-Jalālaīn* of al-Suyūṭī, and *al-Muḥallā* (Maṭba'at Muṣṭafā al-Bāb al-Ḥalabī, Egypt, 1358/1939). Also the same commentary on the margin of the Qur'an published by the same Maṭba'ah, 1344 H.

Bayān al-Qur'ān—M. Ashraf 'Ali Thanawi (Ashraf al-Maṭābi', Thana Bhawan U.P., India).

Al-Durr al-Manthūr fī al-Tafsīr bi al-Ma'thūr—Jalāl al-Dīn 'Abd al-Raḥmān bin Abī Bakr al-Suyūṭī, (possibly published in Egypt).

Fatḥ al-Bayān fī Maqāṣid al-Qur'ān—Ṣiddīq Ḥasan Khān (Maktabat al-'Āṣimah, Cairo, 1307 H.).

Fatḥ al-Raḥmān—Aḥmad bin 'Abd al-Raḥīm (Shah Waliyullah), (Maṭba'ah Fārūqī, Delhi, 1312 H.).

Jāmi' al-Bayān fī Tafsīr al-Qur'ān—Imām Abī Ja'far Muḥammad bin Jarīr al-Ṭabarī (Maṭba'at al-Maymaniyyah, Egypt).

Al-Kashshāf 'an Ḥaqā'iq Ghawāmiḍ al-Tanzīl wa 'Uyūn al-Aqāwīl fī Wjūh al-Ta'wīl—Imām Muḥammad bin 'Umar al-Zamakhsharī (Maṭba'at al-Istiqāmah, Cairo, 1365/1946).

Mafātīḥ al-Ghayb, known as *Al-Tafsīr al-Kabīr*—Imām Fakhr al-Dīn Muḥammad al-Rāzī (Maṭba'at al-'Āmirah al-Sharafiyyah, Egypt, 1308 H.).

Mu'jiz Numā Ḥamā'il Sharīf, with Urdu trans. by M. Ashraf 'Ali Thanawi (Delhi, 1928).

Al-Qur'ān al-Ḥakīm—Urdu trans. by Mufti Shah Muhammad Ahmad Rida Khan, with marginal commentary by M. Na'im al-Din (Taj Company, Ltd. Lahore/Karachi).

Qur'ān Majīd Mutarjam wa Muḥashshah—Urdu trans. by Mahmud al-Hasan with marginal commentary by M. Shabbir Ahmad 'Uthmani (Bijnore, 1952).

Qur'ān, The Holy—Arabic text with Eng. Trans. and commentary by M. Muhammad 'Ali (6th ed., Lahore, 1973).

Qur'ān, The Holy—Arabic text with Eng, trans. and commentary by 'Abdullah Yusuf 'Ali (Lahore, Sh. Muḥammad Ashraf).

Rūḥ al-Ma'ānī fī Tafsīr al-Qur'ān al-'Aẓīm wa al-Sab' al-Mathānī—Abī al-Faḍl Shihāb al-Dīn, al-Sayyid Maḥmūd al-Ālūsī al-Baghdādī (Idārat al-Ṭibā'ah al-Munīriyyah, Egypt).

Tafsīr 'Abdullah ibn 'Abbās (Urdu) with *Lubāb al-Nuqūl fī Asbāb al-Nuzūl* of al-Suyūṭī and trans. of the Qur'an into Urdu by Mawlana Ashraf 'Ali Thanawi (Maṭba'ah Sa'īdī, Kalam Company, Karachi).

Al-Tafsīr al-Kabīr known as *Al-Baḥr al-Muḥīṭ*—Athīr al-Dīn Abī 'Abdullah Muḥammad bin Yūsuf bin 'Alī bin Yūsuf bin Ḥayyān al-Andalusī al-Gharnāṭī al-Jayānī, known as Abī Ḥayyān (Maktabat wa Maṭabi' al-Naṣr al-Ḥadīthah, Riyadh).

Tafsīr al-Qur'ān al-'Aẓīm—H. 'Imād al-Dīn Abū al-Fidā', Ismā'īl bin Kathīr (Dār Iḥyā' al-Kutub al-'Arabiyyah, 'Īsī al-Bābī al-Ḥalabī, Egypt).

Tafsīr al-Qur'ān al-Ḥakīm—al-Shaykh Maḥmūd Shaltūt (Dār al-Qalam, Egypt, 1966).

Tafsīr al-Qur'ān al-Ḥakīm, known as *Tafsīr al-Manār*—al-Sayyid Muhammad Rashīd Riḍā (Maṭba'at al-Manār, Egypt, 1349/1931).

Tafsīr al-Qur'ān al-Jalīl, entitled *Lubāb al-Ta'wīl fī Ma'ānī al-Tanzīl*—'Alā' al-Dīn 'Alī bin Muḥammad bin Ibrāhīm al-Baghdādī, known as al-Khāzan.

Tafsīr al-Qur'ān—M. Shabbīr Ahmad 'Uthmani.

Tafsīr Mūḍiḥ al-Qur'ān—Mawlana Shah 'Abd al-Qadir (Maṭba'ah Khādiman al-Islam, Delhi) and also on margin of *Fatḥ al-Raḥmān Tarjumān al-Qur'ān*—Aḥmad bin 'Abd al-Raḥīm (Shah Waliyullah) (Maṭba'ah Fārūqī, Delhi, 1312 H.).

Tafsīr Rūḥ al-Bayān—al-Shaykh Ismā'īl Ḥaqqī Burūsawī (al-Maṭba'ah al-'Uthmāniyyah).

Tarjumān al-Qur'ān—Abul Kalam Azad (Sh. Mubarak Ali, Lahore).

Ḥadīth Literature

Fatḥ al-Bārī—Abū al-Faḍl Shihāb al-Dīn Aḥmad bin 'Alī bin Muḥammad bin Ḥajar al-'Asqalānī (al-Maṭba'ah al-Bahiyyah al-Miṣriyyah, 1378 H.).

Jāmi' Tirmidhī Sharīf—Arabic-Urdu—Na'ib Husain Naqwi and M. Muhammad 'Ali (Sh. Ghulam Ali & Sons, Lahore, 1963).

Kanz al-'Ummāl—Shaykh 'Alā al-Dīn 'Alī Muttaqī—Urdu trans. by S. Farīd al-Dīn *alias* Achche Miān (Rampur, 1964).

Mishkāt al-Maṣābīh—Walī al-Dīn Muḥammad Khaṭīb 'Umrī—Arabic-Urdu—M. Na'ib Husain Naqwi and M. Muhammad 'Ali (Sh. Ghulam Ali & Sons, Lahore, 1964).

Al-Musawwā min Aḥādīth al-Muwaṭṭa' (al-Maṭba'ah al-Salafiyyah, Makkah, 1353 H.).

Al-Muwaṭṭa'—Imām Mālik bin Anas al-Aṣbahī (Egypt).

Naṣb al-Rāyah li Aḥādīth al-Hidāyah—'Allāmah Jamāl al-Dīn Abī Muḥammad 'Abdullah bin Yūsuf al-Ḥanafī al-Zayla'ī (Dābhīl, Surat, India).

Ṣaḥīḥ al-Bukhārī—Arabic-Urdu—M. Na'ib Husain Naqwi and M. Muhammad 'Ali (Sh. Ghulam Ali & Sons, Lahore, 1963).

Ṣaḥīḥ al-Bukhārī—(Aṣḥaḥ al-Maṭabi' Kutub Khānah-i Rashīdiyyah, Delhi, 1376 H.: also Aṣḥaḥ al-Maṭābi' Nūr Muḥammad, Karachi, 1381/1961).

Ṣaḥīḥ Muslim—(Maṭba'at Muṣṭafā al-Bāb al-Ḥalabī, Cairo, 1377/1958).

Sharḥ Ma'ānī al-Āthār—Abū Ja'far al-Ṭaḥāwī (Maṭba'at al-Muṣṭafā'ī, Delhi).

Sunan Abū Dāwūd (Maktabat Muṣṭafā Muḥammad, Cairo, 1950).

Sunan, al-Kubrā—Abī Bakr Aḥmad ibn Ḥusayn al-Bayhaqī (Maktabah Rahīmiyyah, Deoband).

Sunan al-Nasā'ī (Maktabat al-Salafiyyah, Lahore, 1376 H.); also with *Sharḥ* of Jalāl al-Dīn al-Suyūṭī (al-Maṭba'ah al-Miṣriyyah, al-Azhar).

Sunan Ibn Mājah (Maṭba'ah Mujtabā'ī, Delhi, and Aṣḥaḥ al-Maṭābi' Nūr Muḥammad, Karachi).

Talkhīṣ al-Bukhārī—Arabic-Urdu—Ra'is Ahmad Ja'fari (Sh. Ghulam Ali & Sons, Lahore, 1965–1966).

Tarjumān al-Sunnah—M. Badr 'Alam Nadawi (Delhi, 1367/1948).

'Umdat al-Qārī Sharḥ Ṣaḥīḥ al-Bukhārī—Badr al-Dīn Abī Muḥammad Maḥmūd bin Aḥmad al-'Aynī al-Ḥanafī (Dār al-Ṭibā'ah al-'Āmirah, Egypt).

Fiqh

Aḥkām al-Murtadd fī al-Sharī'ah al-Islāmiyyah—Nu'mān 'Abd al-Razzāq al-Sāmarā'ī (al-Dār al-'Arabiyyah lī al-Ṭibā'ah wa al-Nashr wa al-Tawzī', Beirut, Lebanon).

Aḥkām-i Shar'iyyah min Ḥālāt wa Zamānah kī Ri'āyat—M. Muhammad Taqi Amini (Sind Sagar Academy, Lahore, 1969).

Al-Baḥr al-Rā'iq Sharḥ Kanz al-Daqā'iq—Ibn Nujaym al-Miṣrī (1st ed., al-Maṭba'ah al-Miṣriyyah).

Al-Hidāyah ma'a al-Kifāyah (Maṭba'ah Aḥmadī, Delhi).

Al-Hidāyah, with marginal glosses by Muḥammad Ḥasan al-Sunbulī (Newal Kishore, 1303/1884).

Ḥujjat Allāh al-Bālighah—Shah Waliyullah Dihlawi—Urdu trans. by M. 'Abd al-Rahim (Qawmī Kutub Khānah, Lahore, 1953).

Al-Islām, 'Aqīdah wa Sharī'ah—Shaykh Maḥmūd Shaltūt (2nd ed. Maṭba'at Dār al-Qalam, Cairo).

Islām kā Nizām-i Mahāṣil, Urdu trans. by Nijatullah Siddiqi, of Imām Abū Yūsuf's *Kitāb al-Kharāj* (Maktabah Chiragh-i Rah, Karachi, 1966).

Jāmi' al-Fawā'id min Jāmi' al-Uṣūl wa Majma' al-Zawā'id—Imām Majd al-Dīn Abī al-Sa'ādah al-Mubārak bin Muḥammad bin al-Athīr al-Jazrī al-Mūṣalī (1346 H.)..

Kitāb al-Āthār—Imām Muḥammad al-Shaybānī—Urdu trans. by Abu al-Fath Muhammad Saghir al-Din (Maktabah Sa'īdī, Karachi).

Kitāb al-Muqaddimāt al-Muhdāt li Bayān mā Iqtaḍthū—al-Rusūm al-Mudawwanah min Aḥkām al-Sharī'ah wa al-Taḥṣīlāt al-Muḥkamāt li Ummahāt Masā'ilaha al-Mushkilā—Ibn Rushd, with *Al-Mudawwanāt al-Kubrā* of Imām Mālik.

Kitāb al-Risālah—Imām Muḥammad bin Idrīs al-Shāfi'ī—Urdu trans. by M. Mufti Muhammad Amjad 'Ali (Idārah Taḥqīqāt-i Islamī—Muhammad Said & Sons, Karachi, 1968).

Al-Mabṣūṭ—Shams al-A'immah Abī Bakr Muḥammad al-Sarakhsī (Maṭba'at al-Sa'ādah, Cairo, 1324 H.).

Mabādī' Nizām al-Ḥukum fī al-Islām—Dr 'Abd al-Ḥamīd Mutawallī (Dār al-Ma'ārif, Egypt, 1966).

Al-Mughnī—Abī Muḥammad Muwaffiq al-Dīn bin Qudāmah al-Maqdisī—with marginal notes by al-Sayyid Muḥammad Rashīd Riḍā (3rd ed., Dār al-Manār, Egypt).

Musallam al-Thabūt—M. Muḥibbullah Bihārī (Maktabah Raḥīmiyyah, Deoband, 1109 H.).

Al-Radd 'alā Siyar al-Awzā'ī—Abū Yūsuf (Hyderabad).

Sharḥ al-Zayla'ī 'alā Kanz al-Daqā'iq (al-Maṭba'ah al-'Āmiriyyah, Būlāq, Egypt, 1313 H.).

Sharḥ Fatḥ al-Qadīr—al-Shaykh al-Imām Kamāl al-Dīn Muḥammad al-Siwīsī al-Iskandarī, known as Ibn al-Hummām al-Ḥanafī—*'Alā al-Hidāyah, Sharḥ Bidāyat Mubtadī* of Shaykh al-Islam Burhān al-Dīn 'Alī al-Marghinānī, and on its margin *Sharḥ al-'Ināyah 'alā al-Hidāyah* by Akmal al-Dīn Muḥammad bin Maḥmūd al-Bābartī, and notes by Sa'dullah bin al-'Aynī known as Sadī al-Chalpī (al-Maṭba'ah al-Kubrah al-'Āmiriyyah, Būlāq, Egypt, 1316 H.).

Tarjumān al-Sunnah—M. Badr 'Alam Nadwi (Maṭba'ah Delhi, 1367/1948).

Al-Tashrīḥ al-Janā'ī al-Islāmī—'Abd al-Qādir 'Ūdah (Maṭba'at al-Madanī, al-Mu'assasah al-Sa'ūdiyyah bi Miṣr, 1379/1959).

Al-Tawḍīḥ wa al-Talwīḥ—'Ubaydullah wa Mas'ūd bin 'Umar *alias* Sa'd al-Taftazānī (Newal Kishore, 1353 H.).

History and Miscellaneous

A'zam al-Kalām fī Irtqā' al-Islām—Urdu trans. by M. 'Abd al-Haqq of *Proposed Political, legal and Social Reforms under Muslim Rule* by Nawab A'zam Yar Jang (Maṭba'ah Mufīdī 'Ām, Agra, 1910).

Dā'irah Ma'ārif Islāmiyyah (University of Punjab, 1971).

Early Development of Islamic Jurisprudence, The—Ahmad Hasan (Islamic Research Institute, Islamabad, 1970).

Encyclopaedia of Islam (Leyden, 1932).

Al-Fakhrī fī al-Ādāb al-Sulṭāniyyah wa al-Duwal al-Islāmiyyah—Muḥammad bin 'Alī Ṭabāṭabā' known as Ibn al-Ṭiqṭiqā—ed. By W. Ahlwardt (Griefawald), 1958: its Urdu trans. by Mawlana Muhammad Ja'far Shah Phulwarwi (Idārah Thaqāfati Islamiyyah, Lahore, 1962).

Al-Fawz al-Kabīr—Hujjat al-Islam H. Shah Waliyullah Dihlawi—Urdu trans. by Muhammad Salim 'Abdullah (Urdu Academy Sind, Karachi, 1960).

Ḥayāt Muḥammad—Muḥammad Ḥusayn Haykal—Urdu trans. as *Sīrat al-Rasūl* by Muhammad Warith Kamil (Maktabah Kārwān, Karachi, 1964).

History of Muslim Philosophy, A, ed. M.M. Sharif, Vol, II (Otto Harrassowitz, Wiesbaden, 1966).

Imām Abū Ḥanīfah: Life and Work—Eng. Trans. of Shibli Nu‘mani's *Sīrati Nu‘mān,* by Hādī Ḥussayn (Institute of Islamic Culture, Lahore, 1972).

Imām Ibn Taymiyyah—Professor Abū Zahrah (Egypt)—Urdu trans. by Na'ib Husain Naqwi (Sh. Ghulam Ali & Sons, Lahore, 1968).

Islām aur Madhhabī Āzādī—M. Jalal al-Din Shams (Lahore Art Press, Lahore 1930).

Islām aur Masīḥiyyat—Mawlana Abu al-Wafa' Thana'allah Amristrai (Dīn Muḥammad Press, Lahore, 1960).

Islamic Methodology in History—Dr Fazlur Rahman (Central Institute of Islamic Research, Karachi, 1965).

Al-Kāmil—Ibn al-Athīr—Urdu trans. by M. Maqsud ‘Ali Khayrabadi (Dā'irah Mu‘īn al-Ma‘ārif, Karachi, 1965).

Law of Apostasy in Islam, The—Rev. Samuel M. Zwemer (Marshall Bros., Ltd., London, 1924).

Madhhab kī Nām par Khūn—Mirza Tahir Ahmad (1963).

Maqālāt-i Sir Sayyid, Vol. II (Majlisi Taraqqī Adab, Lahore, 1961).

Mas'alah-i Ijtihād—M. Muhammad Hanif Nadwi (Idārahi Thaqāfāti Islamiyyah, Lahore 1952).

Al-Mizān al-Kubrā—Abū al-Muwāhib ‘Abd al-Wahhāb ibn Aḥmad bin ‘Alī al-Anṣārī al-Shāfi‘ī al-Miṣrī al-Ma‘rūf bi al-Sha‘rānī (Dār Iḥyā' al-Kutub al-‘Arabiyyah, ‘Īsī al-Bābī al-Ḥalabī, Egypt).

Murtadd kī Sazā Islāmī Qānun min—Sayyid Abul A‘la Mawdudi (4th ed., Islamic Publications, Lahore, 1963).

Muslim Conduct of State—Dr Muhammad Hamidullah (5th ed., Sh. Muhammad Ashraf, Lahore, 1966).

Principles of Public International Law—S. Faruq A. Hassan (Lahore, 1972).

Qatl-i Murtadd aur Islām—Mawlawi Sher Ali (Qadian, 1925).

Qatl-i Murtadd, Ghulām aur Laundiyān—M. Ghulam Ahmad Pirviz (Idārah Ṭulū‘i Islam, Lahore).

Qatl-i Murtadd—Mawlana Abu al-Jalal Nadwi A‘zamgarhi (Maṭba‘ah Ḥakīm Barham, Gorakhpur).

Religion of Islam—Mawlana Muhammad ‘Ali (Aḥmadiyyah Anjuman Ishā‘at-i Islam, Lahore, 1936).

Ṣiddīq-i Akbar—Mawlana Sa‘id Ahmad Akbarabadi (Nadwat al-Muṣannifīn, Delhi, 1961).

Sīrat al-Nabī—Shaykh Abī Muḥammad ‘Abd al-Mālik ibn Hishām (Maktabat al-Rabī‘, Ḥalab, Syria)—ed. by Muḥammad Rawās; also its Urdu trans. by M. Qutub al-Din Ahmad Mahmudi (Dār al-Ṭab‘ ‘Uthmāniyyah, Ḥyderabad Deccan, 1949).

Six Lectures on the Reconstruction of Religious Thoughts in Islam—Dr Sir Muhammad Iqbal (Kapur Art Printing Works, Lahore, 1930).

Siyāsī Wathīqah Jāt—Dr Muhammad Hamidullah—Urdu trans. by Abu Yahya Imam Khan Nuwshihrawi (Majlisī-i Taraqqī Adab, Lahore, 1960).

Ta’rīkh al-Rusul wa al-Mulūk—Abū Ja‘far Muḥammad ibn Jarīr al-Ṭabarī—Urdu trans. by Sayyid Muhammad Ibrahim Nadwi (Karachi, 1967): also Arabic text ed. by M.J. DeGoege (E.J. Brill, 1890—Lugd—Batavia).

War and Peace in the Law of Islam—Majid Khadduri (Johns Hopkins Press, 1955).

Periodicals and Details

Al-Ma‘ārif (Idārah Thaqāfati Islamiyyah, Lahore).

Nawā’-i Waqt (Lahore).

Payghām-i Ṣulḥ (Lahore).

Zamīndār (Lahore).

Index

www.ingramcontent.com/pod-product-compliance
Lightning Source LLC
Chambersburg PA
CBHW020922160726

47993CB00005B/2083